SAFETY SMART STUDENT

STUDENT

The Guidebook for College Student Living

By

Colleen Kenniston

This book is a work of non-fiction. The events and situations are true.

ISBN: 1-4107-7858-4 (e-book)
ISBN: 1-4107-7859-2 (Paperback)

Library of Congress Control Number: 2003095708

This book is printed on acid free paper.

Printed in the United States of America
Bloomington, IN

1stBooks - rev. 01/08/04

Dedication

**Dedicated to
College Student Victims of Crime**

Liability or Warranty Disclaimer

This book is provided to those who want to learn more about how to live more safety in a college environment. The author provides suggestions and guides; however, it is not guaranteed that these suggestions and guides are the most appropriate individual choice or solution to any situation or circumstance. It is not to be assumed that information provided in this book gives the best approach and decision in any and all situations pertaining to personal safety and crime prevention. These guides and suggestions do not guarantee that crime prevention techniques and procedures are assumed, or implied, to be the best solution in every circumstance or situation.

Individual needs, decisions and reactions along with varying situations and circumstances influence individual action and/or reaction to criminal activity. The information provided in this book is not intended to replace professional law enforcement advice. Contact your local law enforcement agency for legal information and more information about local, state and federal laws.

The author and publisher do not, expressed or implied, make any warranty of any kind to the guides and suggestions provided in this book. This book is not intended to give legal advice or use of specific self-defense weapons and techniques. Consult with your local law enforcement agency for such information.

The author and publisher disclaim any responsibility and/or liability for personal or otherwise, any loss, damages, or risks incurred by incidents or consequences, directly or indirectly in association with the any of the contents in this book. This book only provides suggestions and guides.

References and organizations that are mentioned in this book are mentioned for information purposes only. The author does not represent and endorse any specific organization, group or company, nor does it offer any endorsement, or implied endorsement for any organizational enterprise.

CONTENTS

Do if You are Raped, Safety Smart Rape Prevention Guides, Safety Smart Message for Women, Safety Smart Message for Men, The Men's Program, and Sexual Offender/Predator Registration.

What is Stalking? Victimization, Stalkers: Simple Obsession, Love Obsession, Erotomania, False Victim, Cyber, Characteristics of Stalkers, Safety Smart Guides to Deal with a Stalker, and a Final Message about Stalkers

What is Domestic Violence? Who are the Victims of Domestic Violence? Male Victims of Domestic Violence, The Clandestine Crime, Who are the Abusers? The Risk to Stay and Safe Way to Leave the Abuser, Four Powerful "P's", and Safety Smart Guides to Leave the Abuser

What is Sexual Harassment? Are you being Sexually Harassed? Safety Smart Guides To Stop Sexual Harassment

The Number 1 Problem: Alcohol Abuse, Binge Drinking, Alcohol Related Arrests, Illegal Drug Use, Dangerous and Life Threatening Drugs found at College, Drugs: Marijuana, MDMA or Ecstasy, GHB, Rohypnol, Ritalin, OxyContin, Ketamine, PCP, Meth, Cocaine, Heroin, LSD, Inhalants, Steroids, Tobacco, Clean and Clear of Alcohol and Drugs

INTRODUCTION

A NEW EXPERIENCE: COLLEGE LIFE

Leaving home for the first time for college is a new passage for millions of young people each year. It is an exciting and personally challenging time. Yet, along with anticipation of pursuing new hopes and dreams, it is also a time of potential anxiety, uncertainty and fear of the unknown. Being independent and on your own for the first time can be a daunting experience, both academically and socially. In your new role as a college student, you want to achieve academic excellence. The time required for study, research and class attendance sometimes seem overwhelming. You will want to develop and expound on your social skills as a young adult. You may also be working part-time to help finance the necessities of college life. It is all new!

When you leave home, you establish your own standards of personal behavior. The values you learned from past experiences do not stay behind but go with you, as they will be your best source of moral support and will help you deal with challenges that you may not expect. In a college environment you can become a victim of crime, or sustain personal injury from accidental events. You have left a largely protected environment where family, friends, and community have provided you with feelings of comfort and security. You now find yourself a stranger among others in an unfamiliar place. The fear of the unknown can become very real. These circumstances increase your vulnerability to both victimization and accidents. It is necessary to be prepared.

Criminals are opportunists who choose targets that look easy. Some criminals target college students because the criminal perceives students as preoccupied and vulnerable and the criminal does not think students possess the personal safety skills necessary to effectively protect themselves. Criminals have the attitude that they are smarter than you are and can take advantage of you. I have written the *Safety Smart Student* so that you can prove them wrong.

My primary purpose is to help you handle your personal safety more effectively by assessing safety and security conditions within the college environment and taking the necessary steps to protect yourself. I have consolidated many personal safety guides in one book to assist you in living your college life securely. To acquire personal safety skills, you need to know about crimes that actually do occur on college campuses and learn what steps to take and what abilities you need to have to reduce your chances of being victimized. Many people believe that it is always *someone else* who becomes a victim of crime. This fallacy is dangerous because any one of us can become a target at any given moment. Another fallacy is that crimes do not occur on college campuses. This is a dangerous notion because it is unrealistic and can lull you into a state of false security. *The first rule of safety is to pay attention to your surroundings and the people around you.* When you let your guard down your chances of becoming the next victim dramatically increases. The personal safety guides I share with you in the chapters that follow emphasize how you can better protect yourself in a college environment and how to select a college that provides you with ample public safety and security.

The focus of this book is threefold: one, to evaluate college campus safety and security procedures; two, to examine potential behavior patterns of the college students which allow predators to target and victimize you as a college student, and three, to provide you the step-by-step guides necessary to live safely as a college student. As you read through the chapters, you will learn to detect the common threads that connect victims and criminals, or *predators,* as I will address them. Unfortunately, it is a fact of life that college opens windows of opportunity for criminals to commit crimes. You are going to learn how to close those windows here. I will share with you true stories of crimes that have been committed against college students; we will analyze how the opportunity arose for the crime to occur and seek out solutions to prevent it from occurring again. As these stories are told, solutions will become more apparent, and you will become a more safety conscious individual. I will also provide applicable web sites for additional information on specific topics.

College life offers endless opportunities to expand your mind and nurture your soul. To take full advantage of all that college offers, you need to live in peace and safety. The ability to distinguish between safe and unsafe living conditions and to acquire the needed skills to have control of your own personal safety will significantly decrease your chances of becoming a victim of crime, whether it is having your bicycle stolen or something more serious, such as personal assault. Also, if a criminal does target you, the individual choices and abilities you bring to that situation can have a major influence on how you survive that attempt. Enhanced awareness of your environment, knowledge of how criminals operate, and methods of ensuring your personal safety are the tools that you need to become a more safety conscious person. Let us begin!

Colleen Kenniston

Chapter 1
COMMUNITY & YOUR PERSONAL SAFETY

Ask Yourself: Am I living in a safe community?

ASSESSING CAMPUS AND COMMUNITY
PROTECTIVE SERVICES

When choosing a college to attend, one of the most important considerations, *personal safety*, is often not thoroughly investigated or it is overlooked altogether. In referring to institutions of higher education, the term "college" is used throughout this book. This includes public and private universities, military, and two-year to post-graduate academic institutions. Some of the factors to consider in determining if the college you are considering has a safe environment are public safety organizations, crime statistics, crime prevention programs, and college and community commitment to public safety.

Many citizens perceive campus police to be primarily security guards. Contrary to this supposition, the majority of college campuses in the United States employ sworn law enforcement officers who carry firearms and have state-mandated arrest powers to enforce laws and ordinances. Police patrols operate on a 24-hour, seven-days-a-week schedule. Crime prevention and investigations are primarily during the week during daytime business hours. These services often go beyond daytime hours and offer students evening and weekend crime prevention programs, or to investigate crime. Another resource, victim service advocates, are usually available 24 hours a day, seven days a week. Recognize that not all college campuses have sworn officers protecting the campus and not all campuses have all the divisions mentioned here. Colleges employing security personnel who are not certified law enforcement officers usually have a working partnership with local law enforcement agencies which respond to incidents that involve arrests and other official police matters. Campus public safety and security departments may also have a mutual aid agreement with neighboring city, county and state law enforcement agencies to assist in police situations requiring a greater magnitude of police power.

In 1995, The Bureau of Justice Statistics (BJS) conducted a survey of campus law enforcement agencies serving U.S. campus communities to determine the level of campus law enforcement services provided to college campus communities. BJS surveyed 4-year colleges with a student enrollment population of at least 2500. In the study, of 682 college campuses meeting the criteria, 680 colleges had either a state-regulated police department or a security service providing safety and security. The study reveals that the larger the student population, the more sworn, armed officers provide protective and security services to the campus communities. The study also indicates that more public colleges than private colleges have sworn and armed officers protecting the campus. Sworn officers are state certified and trained to perform multiple police functions. During your college assessment and selection process, find out what type of public safety organization is responsible for providing police protection and services on campus and in the community.

SSS Web reference: For more information about the BJS survey go to web site http://www.ojp.usdoj.gov/bjs/pub/ascii/clea95.txt.

Collective Crime Control Management

Combating campus crime effectively requires collective participation between students and the community. As a new or returning student, you should expect that the community you have chosen to live in have public safety systems in place to augment your safety. The responsibility does not totally fall on the community, as you are expected to be responsible for your own personal protection and safety. Since crime is too immense and complex for one person or agency to totally manage crime prevention and controls, Collective Crime Control Management (C.C.C.M.) is required. Collective Crime Control Management is a strategic process whereby partnerships between individuals, groups and organizations are established to eliminate and/or deal with criminal activity through active participation of both citizens and law enforcement. C.C.C.M. programs also address personal safety education, criminal apprehension, prosecution, and confinement, for the purpose of establishing a crime controlled environment for everyone.

In the past, some college officials have not reported accurate crime statistics to the public. Because no college wants to appear unsafe, some officials have manipulated and misconstrued data on crimes that occur on campus. As a result, there is ongoing pressure directed at college and public safety officials to report crimes that do occur on college campuses. Any criminal activity that affects your safety as a college student is a critical issue when evaluating a college you anticipate attending. Parents expect their sons and daughters to be protected and safe while they attend college. A collegiate institution is not a separate entity in the community; it is an influential and key participant in the community. All colleges need to have available, to you and other students, ongoing crime prevention orientations and personal safety programs designed to educate and assist in living safely while attending college. There is no acceptable excuse for college officials not to report and make available actual and unaltered crime statistics on an annual and continual basis. This includes reporting violent crimes that occur in the community as quickly and accurately as possible. If a serial rapist is operating in a community, all community members, including students attending college in the area, must be made aware of what is going on for personal safety reasons. Do you want to attend a college that is not honest and forthright about campus crime? How can any college combat crime when they are in denial about the type and number of crimes occurring on campus and in the surrounding community? How can you, the college's most important customer, intelligently assess the safety of your environment when you do not know what is going on? You have to know actual campus crime statistics to help assess your personal safety. You will need this information, so ask questions.

What campus areas are experiencing the most criminal activity? What specific types of crimes are occurring in those areas? What steps are being taken to prevent crime and what programs have been successful in preventing and reducing crime in the local and campus jurisdictions? The best source for this information is the police department's crime prevention or community service department. Inquire about crime analysis, crime mapping and crime prevention programs. Your personal safety assessment of the college you are considering should provide you with pertinent information about what is actually occurring in the college environment, and the effectiveness of the community's Collective Crime Control Management process.

Since you will be living and actively participating both on campus and in the community, visit the local police department and sheriff's office and request community crime statistics. Ask in-depth questions about the neighborhoods where you are looking for a house or apartment. Information should include statistical data on the criminal activity reported in the neighborhood, what types of crimes are occurring, who is committing the neighborhood crime, where, when and how often crime occurs in the area. (Further discussion about student residential living is found in Chapter Three). If you frequent nightclubs and other places where alcohol is available, ask police officials about what problems and crimes are occurring in these local establishments, such as assault and battery, affray (fights involving several people), drug use, and underage drinking. The more these types of incidents occur in nightclubs and other social establishments, the greater your risk of becoming a victim of violent crime.

Campus Safety and Security

The loss of a child is the most devastating, tragic situation any family can ever endure. Accidental death is traumatic enough, and homicide is even more so. A preventable death as a result of a heinous murder is an unbearable situation that brings pain, loss and devastation to the loved ones left behind. The feeling of loss extends to other students attending the college and citizens within the community. Collectively, we need to do everything possible to lessen the possibility of tragedy striking you and your friends and family. Remember the fallacy: *we think others, not ourselves, become victims of crime, but reality proves that any one of us can become a victim at any given moment.*

In 1986, Jeanne Clery, a 19-year-old freshman was raped and murdered in her dorm room on campus. Someone had left the door propped opened which allowed her assailant to enter the dorm. These crimes were not committed by an outsider, but by another student.

The death of Jeanne Clery resulted in a campus safety and security campaign that has compelled colleges receiving federal funds to report campus crime. As a result of dedicated efforts spearheaded by her family, and by citizens like the parents of Jeanne, the U. S. Congress passed the Student Right-To-Know and Campus Security Act, which President George H. Bush signed into law on November 8, 1990. There have been other significant strides over the last few years to require public reporting of crimes that occur on college campuses throughout the United States. In addition to the Student-Right-to-Know and Campus Security Act, Congress enacted the Campus Sexual Assault Victims' Bill of Rights in 1992. Under the Higher Education Act of 1992, reported rape statistics were required to include forcible and non-forcible sex offenses. In 1998, President Bill Clinton signed an amendment changing the name of the Student Right-To-Know and Campus Security Act to the "Jeanne Clery Disclosure of Campus Security Policy and Campus Crime Statistics Act." The amended act requires that a crime log listing crimes that occur daily on campus be made available to the public. This log is available at the campus police department and usually is assessable at the police department's information desk located in the reception area at the patrol division.

The "Jeanne Clery Disclosure of Campus Security Policy and Campus Crime Statistics Act" stipulates that crime statistics for three consecutive years, on any given campus, be made available to the public on an annual basis. You are entitled to receive a copy of this campus crime report publication. This historical profile of improvements in reporting criminal activity reflects an on-going commitment to inform the public about criminal activity occurring in our country's college communities. The National Sexual Violence Resource Center, National School Safety Center, U.S. Department of Justice's Office for Victims of Crime, and Office of National Drug Control Policy (ONDCP), are just a few exemplary examples of national organizations that help college students with victimization, and combat crime on college campuses. Chapter 16 provides additional contact information for victim service resources and information.

SSS Web reference: The Federal Campus Security and Crime Statistics web site is http://www.ope.edu.gov/security. For more information about reporting campus crime go to web site, http://www.ope.edu.gov/security/search.asp.

SSS Web reference: Security On Campus, Inc. web site can be found at, http://www.campussafety.org. This site provides information about campus crime and safety.

Below you will find a list of crimes that are included in the campus crime report. In addition to these crimes, illegal weapons possession, and alcohol and drug use information are reported. Since 1999, non-campus properties, to include nearby streets and sidewalks bordering the college, have been added to the campus crime report. Criminal activities occurring in fraternity and sorority houses located both on and off campus are included in the campus crime report.

The crime categories listed below are the crimes that are mandated for publication under the Clery Act.

Homicide:
* Murder and Non-negligent Manslaughter
* Negligent Manslaughter
Sex Offenses:
* Forcible
* Non-forcible
Robbery
Aggravated Assault
Burglary
Motor Vehicle Theft
Arson
Hate Crimes

Each state has its own state laws and legal definitions. For the purpose of consistency and uniformity, the definitions used by colleges reporting campus crime statistics and the definitions used in this book are from the Federal Bureau of Investigations (FBI)

Uniform Crime Report (UCR). The crimes listed that include the compilation of data in the campus crime report can be used to evaluate reported crimes on and around a college campus. The reliability of this data is dependent on college officials' truthfulness and/or accuracy in data collection and the reporting processes. Issues of reliability and credibility of the data reported have been and continue to be questioned by concerned citizens, since inaccurate information is useless in a personal safety assessment process when selecting a college to attend.

In the past, campus crime statistics encompassed only crimes that victims reported directly to the police. This standard has changed to include crimes of violence reported to police and other college officials. Since 1990, the Jeanne Clery Disclosure Act has helped students and parents get the information they need to assess the safety of a campus environment. Knowing campus crime statistics is necessary to help educate and inform you about personal safety matters, and the dangers that exist in the college and community environment where you will live and learn.

Campus Student Safety Programs

Campus student safety programs vary from college to college. Different programs include: nighttime escort service, residential safety programs, drug and alcohol programs, self-defense classes (Rape Aggression Defense), property identification programs, theft prevention, traffic safety programs, and overall personal safety programs that are designed to help you and other students live safely in a college environment. Available personal safety programs should be noted in your college assessment and selection process. Most campus safety and security departments offer informative web sites that list and describe protective services and crime prevention programs designed for college students.

When you visit a prospective college, be aware of several key considerations while you walk around campus and as you meet with college officials. Notice for example, how a campus will look much different during the day than it does at night. Walking or driving around campus during the day does not show you how well or poorly lit the campus is, and nighttime illumination is important to your personal safety. College officials need to provide well-lit areas, and emergency phones throughout the campus for your safety. The Safety Smart College Student's Checklist at the end of this chapter will assist you with the college safety and security assessment process. Use the checklist to note your findings for the colleges you are considering. Your ability to observe and inquire about the multiple public safety issues that impact your personal safety will improve the quality of your college experience.

Personal Safety Campus Assessment Checklist

The overall commitment to campus public safety by college administrators and public safety officials affects you as a college student. Certain questions should be asked and information gathered before you decide which college to attend. Campus police and the Office of Student Services are two resourceful places you can inquire about campus safety and security issues. The College Student's Personal Safety Campus Assessment Checklist will help you document safety and security issues for the colleges you are seriously considering. With this tool you will be able to compare all the colleges on your list, pinpointing their strengths and weaknesses, and to find out which ones are providing excellence in public safety and security services for their students. You may think of other questions to ask, so have a pen handy to add information to the list. The checklist is subcategorized to include administrative and operational aspects, the campus environment, community services, and safe housing. Before you use the checklist, read each chapter and highlight key safety guides to assist you when using the list.

Parents and students tour the college before the fall semester begins. Did they also walk around the campus at night to assess safety considerations?

The Safety Smart College Student's Checklist

Administrative and Operational Functions

1. Does the college have a public safety department employing sworn officers or non-sworn officers?

( ) State regulated law enforcement agency, employing sworn officers

( ) College public safety department employing non-sworn officers

( ) Contracted security guards

( ) Other _____

2. Are police or security personnel visible during the day and nighttime hours?

( ) Yes ( ) No

Notes:_____

3. Does the college offer 24-hours-a-day, seven-days-a-week police or security coverage?

( ) Yes ( ) No

Notes:_____

4. On average, how long does it take officers to respond to an incident? (The campus police department should have this information).

( ) Less than 5 minutes

( ) More than 5, less than 15 minutes

( ) More than 15, less than 30 minutes

( ) 30 minutes or longer

Notes:_____

5. Know both campus and local police department phone numbers. Local phone books, campus phone directories, college web sites, or campus safety brochures provide this information.

Notes:_____

6. Are college officials publishing and providing crime statistics on an annual basis to the college community? (Reference the Clery Act)

( ) Yes ( ) No

Notes: _____

7. Does the college's police department have a crime prevention unit? Where is it located and what is the phone number and web site?

( ) Yes ( ) No

Notes:_____

8. Does the campus police department have an internal affairs investigation process whereby students can report allegations of police misconduct, or any other public safety concerns directly to the director of campus security? Ask for a pamphlet that explains the process.

( ) Yes ( ) No

Notes: _____

9. Does the college disseminate information to students about the personal safety programs and services available?

( ) Yes ( ) No

Notes:_____

Campus Environment

10. Is the campus adequately lighted at night, to include parking garages, parking lots, buildings, paths and roads?

( ) Yes ( ) No

Notes: _____

11. Does the college maintain well-manicured lawns where shrubbery and trees are trimmed, minimizing isolated areas and maximizing openness where students walk, jog, bike?

( ) Yes ( ) No

Notes:_____

12. Does the campus have emergency phones and blue-lighted phones located throughout campus? Does the campus map include the locations of all emergency phones on campus?

( ) Yes ( ) No

Notes: _____

13. Does the college provide students with ATM locations that are visible, well-lighted and near an emergency phone?

( ) Yes ( ) No

Notes:_____

14. Where are the parking garages and parking lot areas for student use located? Are the parking areas close or far from academic buildings, housing and student activity buildings?

Notes:_____

15. What alternative methods of transportation are available to students who have to park a distance away from campus buildings or who do not have a vehicle?

Notes:_____

16. Are regional or city transit buses available for on-campus and off-campus transportation needs? (Obtain a current route and fee schedule when planning to use the bus system.)

( ) Yes ( ) No

Notes:_____

17. Where are bicycle racks located? Are bicycle racks located in lighted, open areas near academic, residential and student activity buildings?

( ) Yes ( ) No

Notes:_____

18. Are roadways, bike lanes, walkways and parking lots visibly marked to include traffic and parking signs?

( ) Yes ( ) No

Notes:_____

19. Does the college offer a transportation van to accommodate disabled students who need to get to class or other related college activities? (This service is usually located at the college's parking and transportation department.)

( ) Yes ( ) No

Notes:_____

20. Are vehicle decals required to park on campus? (Inquire about cost, parking availability and the parking rules and regulations.)

( ) Yes ( ) No

Note:_____

Community Services Programs

21. Does the college offer personal safety education to students?

( ) Yes ( ) No

Notes: _____

22. Does the college employ nighttime security guards to check campus buildings?

( ) Yes ( ) No

Notes:_____

23. Does the college offer a campus nighttime escort service? (This service can involve both vehicle and walking escorts.)
( ) Yes ( ) No
Notes:_____

24. Does the college offer educational programs about alcohol and drug use, domestic violence, sexual assault, and other violent crimes?
( ) Yes ( ) No
Notes:_____

25. Does the college offer self-defense classes such as Rape Aggression Defense?
( ) Yes ( ) No
Notes:_____

26. Does the college offer students a personal property identification and engraving program?
( ) Yes ( ) No
Notes:_____

27. Does the college provide information on how to report crimes and suspicious incidents?
( ) Yes ( ) No
Notes:_____

28. Does the college offer students crisis intervention and victim services? (Obtain the phone numbers and locations of these services.)
( ) Yes ( ) No
Notes:_____

29. Does the college offer periodic traffic safety education to the campus community?
( ) Yes ( ) No
Notes:_____

Safe Housing

30. What types of residential security measures are in place in student housing? (security personnel, video monitoring surveillance, electronic keys, etc.)
Notes:_____

31. Are residential safety programs given each semester to student residents?
Notes:_____

32. Does the housing facility have a reliable process for distributing keys and a policy regulating key distribution and usage?
( ) Yes ( ) No
Notes:_____

33. Do housing officials or managers inform students about housing rules and regulations?
( ) Yes ( ) No
Notes:_____

34. Inquire about any police reports involving intruders entering housing buildings and rooms to commit crimes such as, theft, sexual assault, alcohol and drug violations.
Notes:_____

35. Harassing phone calls may occur repeatedly when living in residential complexes. Will housing officials help you obtain an unlisted phone number and caller ID?
( ) Yes ( ) No
Notes:_____

36. Are there programs available to help you resolve roommate problems?
( ) Yes ( ) No
Notes:_____

37. Does student housing have solid doors, peepholes, dead bolts, and tightly fitted windows with locks?

( ) Yes ( ) No

Notes: _____

38. Does the college offer a Voluntary Residential Safety Inspection Program?

( ) Yes ( ) No

Notes: _____

39. Does the college offer fire safety and prevention information, hold periodic fire drills, and disburse information on how to be safe during bomb threats and how to handle a bomb threat call?

( ) Yes ( ) No

Notes: _____

Additional
information: _____

_____

_____

_____

_____

_____

Chapter 2
SELF-ESTEEM, INTUITION & INSTINCT

Ask yourself: Do I listen to or ignore my gut feelings?

Self-esteem is a key ingredient in living a responsible life. According to the California Task Force to Promote Self-esteem and Personal and Social Responsibility (1990), "Self-esteem is the likeliest candidate for a social vaccine, something that empowers us to live responsibly and that inoculates us against the lure of crime, violence, substance abuse, teen pregnancy, child abuse, chronic welfare dependency, and educational failure. The lack of self-esteem is central to most personal and social ills plaguing our state and nation as we approach the end of the twentieth century." Self-esteem and confidence are personal characteristics a predator assesses when targeting an individual with the intent to commit a criminal act. Predators are more prone to target individuals with low confidence and low self-esteem so it is essential that you possess and demonstrate a healthy self-esteem and self-confidence as a means of personal safety.

Self-confidence, Self-esteem and Awareness

When considering your personal safety, imagine the predator as a vicious wolf seeking to devour a defenseless lamb. In order to capture its prey, the wolf will look for a lamb that is isolated from the group, moves slower than others, looks weak, is not aware that a wolf is nearby and does not sense danger as well as the other lambs. The consequence for this inattention is a fatal ending. Visualize the vulnerable lamb and the wolf's successful assault. Now visualize a human predator seeking to victimize an oblivious college student. Just like the wolf, the human predator will look for someone who is inattentive and isolated from other people, easily distracted and approachable, receptive to conversation with a stranger, and who projects body language indicative of loneliness, depression or naïveté about dangerous people. The predator is apt to engage such a person in trivial conversation to "size them up," with the intention of victimizing them in the immediate, near or distant future. How would a predator get close to you? Some approaches are to ask you for directions, the locations of popular student hangouts and so on. This gives the predator an opportunity to get close to you to observe and assess your strengths, your level of self-esteem, and your weaknesses and vulnerabilities. Once a predator accomplishes this goal, you are at a serious disadvantage in maintaining your personal safety. But, if you can establish a positive and confident character about yourself, you may avoid giving a predator any information that can be used against you.

Body language and your level of awareness are important considerations in protecting yourself against predators. Without a conscious effort, we do not always pay attention to how we are perceived by others in our everyday interactions and activities. When study demands, exams, work and time with friends absorb our attention, we may not be aware of who or what is around us. We do not realize that others may be assessing our self-confidence and astuteness. The predator is betting that you will not be self-confident and aware of your surroundings. By practicing awareness, learning self-preservation skills and practicing these skills every day, you can outwit the predator.

People react differently to personal attacks. Some people have a tendency to freeze, while others will react in self-defense. How you respond to threats of personal harm will vary according to your personal experiences, perceptions and abilities. Self-preservation requires personal safety skills that will enable you to choose how you are going to react in a potentially dangerous situation. You must be your own best source of protection. This includes being smart about your personal safety, being familiar with your environment, and feeling confident that you can defend yourself when necessary. Your mental and physical abilities affect the criminal's decision to consider you as a potential victim or to let you pass by unharmed. Remember, criminal opportunists think they are smarter than others, and carefully profile a prospective target to avoid detection and failure. Good body language includes maintaining a straight posture - shoulders back, chin and head up, eyes focused on what is in front of you, not on the ground. Use your peripheral vision to observe what is happening around you. These behaviors demonstrate self-confidence and self-esteem to others and discourage criminal opportunists from targeting you. Predators will be inclined to move on to another person who presents a less complicated, easier target.

Body language, also known as *social kinesics*, "telegraphs" your level of self-esteem and self-confidence to others. According to Dr. Albert Mehrabian, 55 percent of your body movements communicate messages to people around you. You need to consciously choose what messages you are sending, since your chances of becoming a victim of crime multiply when you send the message, "I am needy and vulnerable." Predators do not like strength, confidence and unpredictability in their prey. Predators quickly pick up the message that you are smart and know how to take care of yourself when you move with confidence and awareness.

Instincts and Intuition

We have all experienced the "gut feeling" that something is not right at certain times in our life. We have the ability to sense danger. Ignoring our "gut feelings" or "inner sensing" can put us in harms way. Dismissing your instincts and intuition is a big mistake.

Our instincts are unconscious in origin and percolate up to our conscious thoughts. Our intuitions are a more immediate cognitive thought. What exactly are instincts and intuition? Webster's New Collegiate Dictionary defines instinct as, "1: a natural or inherent aptitude, impulse, or capacity"; 2: "behavior that is mediated by reactions below the conscious level". Intuition is "1: immediate apprehension or cognition; a: knowledge or conviction gained by intuition; b: without evident rational thought and inference; 2: quick and ready insight." Cognition is defined as, "the act or process of knowing including both awareness and judgment."

Your goal is to reach the highest level of overall personal safety possible in your daily life. Your instincts and intuition help you expand your cognitive abilities so that you can sense the presence of dangerous people or potential personal harm. *Listen to both your instincts and your intuition.* Paying heed to these warning signals does not mean living in a state of paranoia. Nature has provided us with the ability to sense danger. Making use of your instincts and intuition is both normal and necessary. Paranoia, on the other hand, is "a psychosis characterized by systemized delusions of persecution... a tendency on the part of an individual or group toward excessive or irrational suspiciousness and mistrustfulness of others." Intuition and instinct, your human inner alarm system, is much different than paranoia, which is a state of unreasonable fear. Paranoia debilitates the quality of a person's life, making professional counseling necessary to reestablish a functional lifestyle. Intuition and instincts safeguard the quality of your life. When you have a "bad feeling" about something, be alert to your surroundings and recognize that your inner self is telling you to be careful.

Personal Fitness

A high level of personal fitness will give you the confidence you need to do a good job of taking care of yourself. Visualize a "fitness" triangle divided into three equal parts: mental, physical, and personal safety. Academic studies lead to healthy mental fitness. Participation in athletic activities and fitness programs helps maintain healthy physical fitness. Personal safety fitness requires educating yourself about personal safety practices, being alert to what is around you, projecting an image of self-confidence, detecting the deceptions of others, and avoiding potentially bad social situations. "You" are the center of your own life. Feeling good about yourself and taking care of your mind and body help shield you from potential victimization. Being self-confident, liking yourself and living safely are essential to a healthy life. Make self-confidence, self-esteem, safety and security your everyday experience.

Students engaged in their academic and social activities

Chapter 3
ON-CAMPUS & OFF-CAMPUS RESIDENTIAL LIVING

Ask yourself: Am I safe in my home?

As a college student, you will choose either on-campus or off-campus housing. Living on-campus is popular for many first and second year students and married students with children. Many students in their junior, senior and graduate years prefer to live in off-campus apartments or private homes with friends. Your decision to live either on or off campus will require you to consider a number of issues in deciding where you will live and with whom.

Whether you live in a residence hall or lease an apartment, your signature on a contract signifies your acceptance of the rules and regulations expected of you and your roommates as occupants of a residential dwelling. Rental agreements and leases are designed to protect tenants and their property. Your knowledge, acceptance and compliance with the terms of the leasing agreement will help maintain a safe living environment for you and your living companions. In addition to your signing a rental agreement, you should also be provided with residential security features to maximize your safety and security. Some of these features include home alarm devices, tightly installed windows with secondary locking devices, solid doors with dead bolts, security personnel, personal safety programs and information.

ON-CAMPUS LIVING

On-campus living offers a variety of choices including family housing, village apartments, residence halls or dormitories, and fraternity and sorority houses. On-campus housing facilities each have their own unique accommodations, however, security issues are applicable to all of them. To insure your own personal safety in on-campus housing, learn and abide by the safely rules and regulations on your housing contract.

Know the Rules

The main concerns in residential policy are safety and student conduct. Housing rules and regulations inform students about the prohibition of firearms or other weapons, use of alcohol and drugs, smoking, noise, disorderly conduct, destruction of property, parking, bicycles, roller blades, skateboards, motorcycles and autos.

People in possession of firearms and explosive devices near or in any public building continue to be an increasing concern to public welfare. Firearms are prohibited on college campuses. Some of you may have weapons for sporting purposes or other legal activities, but safety smartness mandates not being in possession of a firearm or any weapon on a college campus. Keep your personal weaponry home.

Housing rules are also established to manage and deal with inappropriate behavior and misconduct. Inappropriate behavior that disturbs others in a housing complex on a consistent basis will most likely put you out of a place to live. You could also be referred to the student judicial affairs office for possible sanctions. Housing officials should provide you with housing rules and regulations so that you will know what behaviors are acceptable or not acceptable, and what others can do and can not do. Prohibited behaviors include, but are not limited to, disorderly conduct, harassment, affrays (fights), pranks that may cause personal injury, and throwing objects that have the potential to harm others. Prohibited behaviors may also involve threats, intimidation or abuse and can be carried out in various ways. Chapters 7, 9, and 14 discuss some of these problem behaviors, such as obscene or harassing phone calls, stalking, and hazing. Hate crimes are included under discrimination and intimidation behavior that displays prejudice toward race, religion, ancestry, sexual orientation, national origin, or ethnicity.

Handling Roommate Problems

Unless you request a specific roommate or a room by yourself, campus housing officials will assign you to a specific room or apartment with other students. Getting compatible roommates is usually based on luck, unless you are rooming with a friend. Resident advisers are on staff to help students with roommate problems and other residential needs. Usually, you and your new roommates are strangers to one another. It is natural that you will "size each other up" as far as; likes, dislikes and personal behaviors are concerned. How well or poorly you and your roommates get along and whether your different personalities are compatible is important to be able to live in harmony and maintain a safe lifestyle. Roommate relationships impact our personal lifestyle and can affect our ability to succeed in our educational goals. Different lifestyles, norms and values abound in college housing. Conflict and turmoil are common when one roommate is focused on studying and avoids drugs and alcohol, while the other roommate keeps late hours, indulges in drugs and/or alcohol avoids study or brings home strangers. What can you do when you find yourself in such a predicament, which is potentially unsafe as well as unpleasant? The first step is to talk with your roommate to express and communicate your concerns and expectations about living together. When you do not feel comfortable or confident that talking to your roommate will resolve the problem, an alternate solution is to immediately report any inappropriate behaviors to the residence hall advisor or housing director for resolution. Resolution can lead to reconciliation when the roommate's bad behavior ceases, or to change roommates when necessary. Any illegal activity needs to be reported to campus law enforcement. You do not have to remain in a situation where disruptive, dangerous or illegal practices of others affect your personal safety and the quality of your college experience. You have the right to live in a safe and comfortable atmosphere while you are attending college.

Colleen Kenniston

Live as a Team

It is not always easy for you to maintain a safe environment when hundreds of students are sharing a residential complex with you. The more people sharing a residential complex, the harder it is to monitor and control the safety aspects that are required to maximize your personal safety and the safety of the community as a whole. Students that practice leaving doors and windows unsecured, present an opportunity for intruders to gain access to their building and also to individual rooms. Leaving either your individual door or the building's door unlocked or propped open for anyone to enter endangers you, your roommates and everyone else in the building. Allowing non-residents into a residential building creates opportunity for crime. Police incident reports show that unknown males have entered unlocked rooms of female residents while they slept. *Lock your door when you are not in your room and also when you are in your room*, regardless of your gender. Remember, crime can happen to anyone at any time. Both men and women must safeguard themselves from unwanted and potentially dangerous intrusion.

No single effort, by itself, can sustain a safe environment. Your participation, along with other students, and college officials, must work together as a proactive team to maintain safety in your residential housing. Some on-campus residence halls and dormitories provide residents with electronic keys and have surveillance monitoring devices located in strategic areas inside and outside the buildings to guard against crime. Housing security personnel also patrol the area around residence halls. In addition, campus police officers or security guards conduct security checks around the outer areas of housing complexes owned by the college. Still, with all these safeguards in place, you need to lock the doors of the building and the room you live in at all times to deter an intruder from getting into the building and into your room.

Housing security staff and video surveillance devices are also effective methods of crime deterrence and detection. Look for these features when you choose a place to live. Be aware of the behaviors of other residents. Neighboring resident students who permit strangers to enter the building and do not secure their living areas and rooms can impact and affect the safety of your living environment. Criminal

26

opportunists look for open windows and unlocked doors. The criminal choice is the "easy target". A safe and smart student never makes it easy for a predator to enter his or her living space to steal or inflict bodily harm. How you control your keys, lock your doors, report suspicious persons and incidents to police, and keep intruders out of the building helps determine whether or not a crime will occur in your living environment.

Although dorms, residence halls, and on-campus apartment complexes have housing staff in the building's lobby or office to assist residents and monitor who goes in and out of the building, no one can expect housing staff to observe everything that is going on. You have to do your part in protecting where you live. Since all housing residents are provided keys to the building, their floor and individual rooms, it is important that you control your key so that no one else has access to it. When you have guests in the building, it is your responsibility to register them with the housing office staff and remain with them while they are in the building. Housing policy prohibits keys from being lent or given to others. When you give your key to someone else, you have lost control over your personal safety. *Safety smartness involves having possession of your key at all times.*

Always have your key in your hand when approaching your building and visually scan the area as you walk toward the building, especially at night. If you do not have your key in your hand when you approach your building, you are not able to gain immediate access to the building. In situations when you do not have your key at all, and must wait for someone else to let you into the building, you are even more vulnerable. Criminals wait for these opportunities. If your key is lost or stolen, immediately report the missing key to the resident advisor or housing staff.

Many college campuses have emergency and/or blue-lighted phones located around the residential campus complexes, academic buildings, student activity buildings, parking lots, garages, and walkways. Become familiar with their locations and use them when you need help.

Who's Who

Become familiar with who is living in the residential complex and on your floor. Because residents see each other in the building on a regular basis, you will soon recognize who does not belong in the building. Actively participate in keeping your living environment safe by reporting any suspicious persons or activities to police officials. Always avoid confronting an intruder. Campus police will promptly investigate suspicious persons or incidents at your residence hall. The college may also have security guards at your building, so rely on them for your personal safety needs.

FRATERNITY AND SORORITY LIVING

Fraternity and sorority houses differ from other college living arrangements, but the same personal safety standards also apply to them to maintain a safe living environment. Living in a fraternity or sorority house does not eliminate you as a crime victim. Ted Bundy made that clear when he was able to enter a sorority house and clubbed to death a sorority sister.

Sorority sisters many times leave their doors open to allow each other to freely walk in and out of each other's room. *Never leave your doors open or unlocked when you are not there and always keep the outer doors locked.* Giving boyfriends or other non-residents of the house keys or the security code to gain access into the house is a breach of security and potentially dangerous to everyone living in the house.

Fraternity and sorority members often socialize together and become friends. It is important to determine your security needs and establish a team effort to maintain a living environment free from criminal activity.

The House Determines Security Needs

Establishing a good working relationship between the college, the house and law enforcement officials is a necessary effort to maximize your safety and security. Fraternity and sorority members enjoy an active social calendar of parties and other events throughout the year, emphasizing the need to coordinate social events with the campus police to maximize everyone's safety.

Fraternity and sorority houses can also benefit from having an officer conduct a residential safety inspection. This is an on-site safety inspection of the interior and exterior of the house and property. The inspection process is further discussed in the Voluntary Residential Inspection section of this chapter. Working together with college and police officials to maximize safety creates a stronger partnership between house residents and the college, and weakens the criminal's position in targeting the house for a break in or other more dangerous criminal activity.

FAMILY ON-CAMPUS HOUSING

Pursuing a higher education is challenging, time consuming and expensive. Married students, especially those with children have the added responsibility balancing the daily demands of attending classes with the added duty to work and take care of family. Many colleges smooth the path by offering family housing facilities designed to accommodate the unique needs of student families.

If you are a student parent, choosing a safe living environment for your children is of utmost importance. In addition to other needs, children require school transportation during the academic year and supervised after school activities. The district's school bus schedule determines the times your child is picked up and returned home. But, where is your child or children after school? How safe are they when you are not around them? Depending on your child's age, an after school or day care program may be required, unless a relative or close friend can take care of your child. The daily demands that student parents encounter can result in a child being ignored or a parent not being attentive to what is going on in a child's life. Communicating with your child helps you to know how well or poorly your child is doing in school, and what activities and people occupy him or her before, during and after school. Those activities may involve playing with other neighborhood children. As a parent, it is your responsibility to meet with other parents in your neighborhood. Knowing them helps you to be cognizant of who does and who does not belong in the neighborhood. Your ability to be able to identify suspicious individuals and activities in the neighborhood and immediately report suspicious persons and activities to the police will enhance the safety of yours and every other child living in your neighborhood community.

When it comes to protecting our children, drugs continue to be a serious problem without a permanent solution and barriers. Drug dealers operate in and around schools and may be close to your home as well. Keeping drug dealers and other intruders out of your neighborhood and away from your child's school and play areas requires open communication with campus law enforcement officers, college administrators, and housing officials who must join together with parents and children to maintain the safest possible living environment. Most family housing complexes have an on-site staff to coordinate and manage the complex. Get to know these people. Neighbors involved in illegal drug use, domestic violence and other dangerous activities need to be reported to the campus police and housing officials.

The following eight safety guides for family living will help you and your family live in a safer environment.

8 Campus Family Living Guides

Guide 1: Talk to your children and your spouse every day. Know what is going on in their lives.

Guide 2: Become acquainted with neighbors, housing staff and campus police.

Guide 3: Report suspicious activities or persons immediately to the police.

Guide 4: Participate in a neighborhood crime watch program.

Guide 5: Keep your doors and windows locked and do not let strangers into your home. Teach your children to take the same precautions you do.

Guide 6: Most family housing complexes do not have garages where you can park your car, motorcycle or bicycle for safekeeping. Lock your bicycle with a U-lock and use well-lighted bicycle racks, or keep your bicycle inside your home. The habit of always locking your car door and never leaving the keys in your car helps deter auto theft. A car alarm is a plus in deterring auto theft. More information about auto theft prevention is found in Chapter Five.

Guide 7: Family housing complexes usually include a laundry room for resident use that is equipped with coin-operated washers and dryers. Coin-operated machines, or coin machines are targets for criminals, who break into the machines to steal the coins. When no one is in the laundry room and someone has left the door propped open or a window open, the criminal has his or her best chance to commit a crime. Coins, clothing and anything else left behind in a laundry room are up for grabs to a criminal opportunist.

Guide 8: Safe living requires everyone to work together to deter criminal activity in your neighborhood and community.

OFF-CAMPUS LIVING

Off-campus housing is another alternative to campus residential halls, dormitories or on-campus apartments. Many newer off-campus apartment complexes and renovated complexes offer three and four bedroom apartments where each person has their own bedroom and bathroom, but share a common living and kitchen area. Selecting roommates in these situations is an important decision. Many apartment managers offer a roommate matching process that is designed to match personalities and lifestyles for compatible living situations.

Law enforcement and property managers or owners often work together to enhance apartment and home safety in off-campus living situations. The Voluntary Residential Safety Program (VRSP) is an example. Law enforcement officers who are certified in residential security conduct residence inspections in cooperation with property owners and college officials. Colleges and communities that offer this service should be given extra credit in your assessment and selection process. It is an excellent program that checks important residential safety factors that are otherwise often overlooked. There is one note of caution: while a rental property may be on the list of approved properties; that does not mean that all apartments are the same. The inspection process does not inspect all apartments. The officer inspects only one of each different type of apartment or residential unit in the complex, presuming the other units are the same. This may or may not be the case. It is important to know then what is included in the program's safety inspection criteria before you make a decision to live in a particular place off-campus.

Residential Safety Inspection Criteria

The inspection process usually involves checking the interior and exterior of a residential structure, including windows, external doors, landscaping, lighting, attic walls, basements and security alarm systems. Rental property that you are considering, however, may or may not participate in the inspection program. In that case, ask the campus police department to conduct an inspection of your rental unit. Find out what safety criteria are being checked and whether the place you plan to live meets the standards of the VRSP program. Apartment complexes that offer security personnel on-site or an electronic gate where a key or code is necessary for access are especially desirable. Although electronic gates enhance the safety of a residential environment, it is easy for a vehicle to follow someone onto the premises, without a key or code, or for someone to walk through the gate when it is opened. Security personnel who monitor and patrol the residential complex area are a definite plus. Closely observe the landscaping, lighting and parking areas. After visiting a residential complex or house during the day, come back at night to assess lighting and parking area suitability. Overgrown trees, shrubs and grass indicate that management is not committed to adequately landscaping the property. Heavy shrubbery near a house or apartment, walkways, and parking areas deter visibility and openness. It is easy for a criminal to hide behind overgrown shrubbery to avoid detection. The same holds true for poor lighting near stairwells, walkways, parking areas and entranceways. Every residence entryway needs to be well illuminated.

Windows and doors come in many sizes and shapes and need to have a primary and secondary locking device. A loose or poorly installed window gives an intruder easier access into your apartment or house. Check the windows for tightness to the window frame. Check the locking system, and make sure the latches are functional. Locking devices will vary depending on the type of window found in a structure. The four different types of windows are sliding, awning, casement, or jalousie. A home improvement store can recommend a secondary locking device for each type of window. Most rental properties have maintenance personnel who can install these locks for you. Even if you have to pay for secondary locks yourself, your personal safety is well worth the price.

If criminals are unable to gain access to your home through a window, they will look for an external door for easy entry. Your doors need to be solid, not hollow, with inside hinges, not outside. Every outside door should have a dead bolt lock that is at least one inch in length. Before opening a door, always know who is on the other side and do not open the door for anyone who is unknown to you. Look out the door's peephole to see who is there. Remember, there are blind spots when looking through a peephole. Sliding glass doors can be pried off its track if it is not properly on the track. Secondary locking devices are suggested for sliding glass doors and other double doors. Blocking devices are available for the upper track of the door to keep the door from being lifted from its track. French doors should also have secondary locks to prevent easy entry.

As part of your assessment, you may notice more safety features such as security alarm systems in each unit, security officers at entrance areas and fencing around the property. The presence of these features, along with the other features discussed, are indicators that the landlord or property manager is attentive in providing you with a safe living environment.

Fire Safety

Many students living together in a residential complex requires that you practice fire safety. When others set paper on fire in a trash container, or display other similar behavior where a fire is started, it creates a potential danger to everyone. Tampering with any fire equipment or setting off fire alarms is unlawful and creates a potentially dangerous circumstance when the equipment is needed to detect or put out a fire. Tampering with on-campus fire apparatus can result in your being arrested, and also student judicial disciplinary action. On campus, it is not permissible to have any flammable liquids or solvents anywhere in a residential building. For more information about housing rules and regulations addressing smoking, use of candles, cooking in rooms, electrical cords, holiday decorations and trees and chemicals allowed in the rooms, ask housing officials before you move in. Find out what is permissible and what is not. *Cooking in rooms and plugging too many electrical cords into an outlet are the two main causes of residential fires in campus residences.*

Responding to a Fire Alarm

Living in a residence hall or dorm will require you to periodically participate in fire alarm drills. When a fire alarm is activated, follow the proper evacuation practices and procedures you have learned. Fires are dangerous and can take the lives of those not prepared to handle such a dangerous situation or those who ignore the early warning alarms. The sound of a fire alarm requires everyone to immediately evacuate the building by using the stairway as the primary exit, *not* elevators. Remaining in your room is a dangerous decision. Quickly respond to the fire alarm warning and evacuate the building in a calm and expeditious manner. Report residential fires immediately by calling 9-1-1. Fire extinguishers and fire alarms are placed around stairwells and hall areas. Become familiar with these locations in your building and learn how to operate a fire extinguisher. For more information about fire safety, ask your resident advisor or apartment manager to have a firefighter conduct fire safety training for your residence.

A Safety Message

To sum it all up: Intruders enter your home to harm you, to steal, or both. The harder you make it for someone to get near or into your home, the safer you are, since most criminals will look for easy targets. Always stay a step ahead of the criminal. Eleven safety guides for practicing residential safety are listed for you.

11 Safety Smart Living Guides

Guide 1: Lock doors and windows to keep dangerous persons out. It only takes a few seconds for someone to access your home or room. An open window or unlocked door is what a criminal is waiting for.

Guide 2: Security alarm systems and secondary locking devices are recommended, in addition to the primary locking device, for both your doors and windows. A hollow door should be replaced with a solid door and hinges should be inside your dwelling, not outside. The door's peephole should have at least a 180-degree view.

Guide 3: If you see or hear suspicious activity around your house or a parked car, call the police. Report suspicious person(s), vehicles and/ or activities. Be prepared to give as much detail as possible to police dispatchers about what you hear or see that is suspicious. This could include a description of the person or vehicle, where the vehicle is parked, a license number if visible, where you hear or see the person, or any other information that can help the police. Find a safe place to stay.

Guide 4: When you are home in the evening, keep your curtains and window shades closed. Do not give anyone the opportunity to watch you, to study your habits, to find out what the inside of your home looks like, what you have on, and whether you are home alone.

Guide 5: Consider the safety of your personal property also. Not only will strangers try to steal your property, but also some of your associates, friends or acquaintances might take whatever they can while in your house or room. Campus and local police departments offer property identification programs. Take advantage of these programs.

Guide 6: When leaving your home for a long weekend, holiday or spring break, secure your property. Make an inventory list of your personal property such as jewelry, electronic equipment and CDs. Take photos of your belongings and keep them stored in a separate place. Some people video-record their property and keep the tape in a safe place.

Guide 7: Your safety from intruders involves mutual cooperation with others and personal accountability. During the academic year the campus police and housing officials offer personal safety programs. Take advantage of these programs and encourage your friends, roommates and neighbors to do so also.

Guide 8: Have your key readily assessable for entering your building and your room or apartment. Before unlocking the door, check to make sure it is not already unlocked unless you are sure your roommate is home. If the door is unlocked or forced open, do not enter your residence. Go to a safe place and call the police. Leaving an extra key under a mat or in a plant on the porch is like leaving the key in the lock for anyone to enter. Criminals look for these advantages.

Guide 9: Well-manicured lawns, shrubbery and well-lighted parking lots, walkways, and entrance areas are a must in maintaining a safe living environment. Before going out for the evening, turn on the outside entrance light.

Guide 10: Participate in your neighborhood crime watch program.

Guide 11: Never let mail, newspapers, or notes taped to the door accumulate while you are gone on vacation or other extended periods of time. Criminals will look for signs that you are out of town so they can burglarize your home. Ask a neighbor or friend to pick up your paper and other deliveries while you are gone, or temporarily cancel your subscriptions to magazines and newspapers.

Chapter 4
TRAVEL SAFELY ON-CAMPUS & OFF-CAMPUS

Ask Yourself: Do I travel safely?

O ur ability to get around campus and around the community, as well as how we manage long distance travel, impacts our quality of life. On a crowded college campus, and in your surrounding community, hundreds to thousands of people are all sharing walkways and roadways throughout the campus property. Cars, motorcycles, bicycles and pedestrians mingle together, requiring a high level of traffic safety to avoid crashes and injuries.

Extend Common Courtesy

Most college campuses have limited roadways and walkways shared by hundreds to thousands of people. The intermingling of pedestrian traffic with all the other methods of transportation can create a chaotic environment that requires strict observance of both traffic and parking laws. Extending courtesy toward one another while sharing roadways and walkways is necessary. Courtesy involves everyone abiding by the traffic laws and the college's parking and transportation rules and regulations. Courtesy also involves being considerate and not cutting in front of someone on the roadway or walkway. When we're in a hurry, other drivers can irritate us by not driving as fast as we think they should. This can lead to "road rage".

"Road rage" has become a major public safety hazard with the potential to cause serious injury and death. "Road rage" is ubiquitous in our country, to include our college communities. "Road rage" is when a driver becomes angry with another driver that results in aggressive behavior that is antagonistic, vengeful, or retaliatory toward the other person on the road. When someone tailgates you, drives too slow, or a bicyclist swerves in front of you, refrain from unnecessary comments, swearing, hand signs or physical con-frontations. Yelling, swearing, giving someone the finger, or getting out of your car and throwing a punch does not solve anything. What it does is create a greater opportunity for fights and personal injury. Abiding by traffic laws, and remaining calm when other drivers, bicyclists or pedestrians are not courteous, is a safety smart practice. Traffic citations and parking tickets are costly, and college is expensive enough without having to expend your limited discre-tionary funds paying off tickets. Be courteous in all your travels and abide by traffic laws and parking rules.

Make the Best of Your Travels

The most popular methods of transportation used by college students include your feet, automobile, motorcycle, scooter, bicycle, and using the regional transit bus system. The automobile is the most common method of getting around town. Walking, biking and taking a bus are often used for on-campus and near-campus travel. These alternative methods of transportation help alleviate the shortage of parking spaces on college campuses. Parking shortages in the inner campus areas close to academic and student service buildings have prompted many colleges to build parking garages and parking lots on the perimeters of the campus, and these may not be the safest places to park, especially at night. It makes sense to ride your bicycle or take the bus to get around campus. Also, you may want to ride a bicycle, or opt to ride a bus to get around campus after parking your car. Motorcycles and scooters are a less frequent but not uncommon methods of transportation for college students. These vehicles must obey traffic laws and parking rules as cars and require the same courtesy to pedestrians and other drivers.

Have Feet Will Travel

Walking and jogging are not only beneficial to your physical fitness, but it gets you where you want to go. As a new student in an unfamiliar college environment, become familiar with the geographic outlay of the campus. Visit the campus before the semester begins to acclimate yourself to your new surroundings. Get a map of the campus so you can locate all campus buildings and roadways. Campus maps are available at checkpoint locations at the periphery of the college campus, at the campus police department, and at other departments that regulate parking, housing and other student services. It is easier to acclimate yourself to the campus when the college is not in full session.

Use Safe Paths

When walking, jogging, or roller-blading, always use well-lighted, visible areas and paths that are designated for this type of transportation. Being safety smart means avoiding dark, isolated areas. Being a safety smart student, you do not compromise your personal safety by giving someone an opportunity to commit a crime against you.

Protection from personal injury is another consideration when walking on-campus and off-campus. Sidewalks, crosswalks and traffic signals contribute to safe travel. Drivers and pedestrians do not always pay attention to where they are going. Be aware of oncoming traffic before you enter a roadway or intersection so you will not be broad-sided by any of the many kinds of vehicles found on a college campus. In addition to autos, bikes, motorcycles and scooters, large trucks enter campus to deliver supplies, furniture and other merchandise. College campuses have narrow roadways where oversized vehicles such as 18-wheelers are a potential safety hazard. When the driver is making a turn, the wheels may go over the curb because the street is too narrow to accommodate a large vehicle. This event, coupled with the conglomerate of people and traffic, is potentially dangerous.

When you see a large truck or bus coming toward you as you stand on the curb of the intersection, step back. You can't be sure the vehicle can make a clear turn without the wheels hitting the curb or you. This is one way students have been killed on campus. Near misses and fender-benders involving bicycles, autos, trucks, buses and pedestrians is a daily occurrence on a college campus. Be smart and practice safety in all your travels.

Motor Vehicles On-Campus

If you plan to have a car, motorcycle or scooter on campus, you are required to register your vehicle with the police department or parking transportation department. Most large colleges have a parking and transportation department that is separate from the campus police department. Smaller colleges usually merge the two functions under the campus police department. Registering an automobile, motorcycle or scooter involves acquiring a parking decal for your vehicle. Many colleges today offer their students an online service where you can purchase your parking decal directly from their website. This is the way to go, instead of waiting in a long line, waiting to purchase a parking decal. A numbered decal displayed on your vehicle allows you to park in designated areas. Obtain a copy of the parking and transportation rules and regulations and become familiar with them, to avoid being plagued with parking tickets.

You may want to consider taking advantage of the regional or city transit system to get to campus. In addition to the city's transportation division, the campus parking and transportation department and the campus police department provide bus routes and fee schedules. The fee for bus transportation to campus is usually a nominal personal expenditure.

How You Can Stay Safe on Road Trips

Several factors are pertinent to safe travel. What do you do when your vehicle breaks down or you encounter an emergency while driving down a roadway? Fortunately, many college students carry a cellular phone and can call for help immediately. If you do not have a cell phone, look for a nearby telephone or call box. What do you do when a mechanical problem or flat tire occurs in an unfamiliar or unsafe area? The first step is to get you and your vehicle out of the way of other traffic to avoid injury or crashes. Start by activating your emergency flashers. When circumstances prohibit you from being able to move your vehicle out of the road, activate your flashers to warn oncoming traffic, and then exit your vehicle safely. Remaining in the vehicle increases your chance of personal injury or fatality if an oncoming vehicle crashes into your vehicle.

What do you do when a stranger approaches you to render assistance? You do not know whether the person is a Good Samaritan or someone trying to take advantage of a vulnerable situation. Once your vehicle is safely parked, away from on-coming traffic, remain in your vehicle with the doors locked while communicating with the would-be helper. This creates a barrier between you and a person you do not know. Do not roll the windows down so far that someone can reach inside your vehicle, open the door, and grab you. The same safety practices apply when you are assisting someone who has a disabled or broken-down vehicle. You can effectively help without getting too close to the person or the vehicle. The person you are attempting to help may or may not be in an authentic emergency, since criminals sometimes use this technique to lure their victims. Remain in your car with the doors locked and, from a safe distance, ask if they want you to call the police or a towing company. Accepting a ride from a stranger places you in a potentially dangerous situation. *Never accept a ride from a stranger*. When you get into a stranger's vehicle, you have lost your advantage and control over your own personal safety.

Driving and Cell Phones

Serious injuries and fatalities occur every day in this country because driving and talking on the phone does not mix well. You can cause a serious accident because you are distracted by a phone conversation. Driving your vehicle takes precedence over talking on the phone. *Remain attentive to your driving instead of drawing your attention to talking on the phone while driving your vehicle*. By making this decision, you are being responsible for your safety and the safety of others as you travel the roadways.

Safety Guides for Parking Your Vehicle

A college newspaper reports a female student who encountered a dangerous predator while getting out of her car in an isolated parking lot near her apartment. This reminds us of potential personal danger in our everyday activities. How do you best safeguard yourself from these types of situations? Park your vehicle in a well-lighted area that is as close to your apartment as possible. Look around before you get out of your vehicle and have your key to the building and your apartment in your hand. Be familiar with other people who use the parking lot, so you will recognize people who do not belong. Do what you have to do to avoid being forced into a vehicle or taken to any isolated place. The situation changes drastically, to the predator's benefit, not yours, once you are forced into a vehicle or dragged to an isolated place. You have a better chance to get away from the predator at the beginning of the encounter. Run, scream, scratch, kick, do whatever you have to do to get away. Personal safety involves getting away from the predator, finding a safe place, and immediately calling the police. Flight is always better than fight, when there is a choice. The ten safety guides listed for you will enhance safe travel on and off-campus.

10 Safety Smart Traveling Guides

Guide 1: Always extend courtesy to others when sharing walkways and roadways. "Road rage" can result in serious traffic accidents and even fatalities.

Guide 2: Whether you drive, bike, walk, jog or roller blade, avoid collisions with others by being constantly aware of what is going on around you, particularly when entering an intersection.

Guide 3: Choose your path wisely. Become familiar with the geographic outlay of the campus and select the best paths that offer the greatest amount of environmental safety. Use roads and walkways that have been designated for the method of transportation you are using. Select paths that are well lit and do not have overgrown shrubbery and stay away from dark and isolated areas. Try to always walk, jog or roller blade with friends and always use open, populated places for these types of travel.

Guide 4: For safe cycling, use the bicycle lanes, avoid going the wrong way on a one-way road, and know the bicycle traffic laws. Bicycles are considered vehicles and state traffic laws apply when you are biking. Have a good light on your bicycle for riding at night, and register your bicycle with the campus or local police department. When you park your bicycle, use a well-lit, visible bicycle rack and lock your bicycle with a good U-lock. These safety guides protect you and your bicycle from injury or theft.

Guide 5: Make room for large vehicles. Beware of large vehicles, such as buses or trucks that travel on narrow campus roads. Avoid being too close to the curb where you can be hit and injured by large vehicles trying to make a turn or go around a corner.

Guide 6: Be prepared for a road emergency. When traveling in your vehicle, an emergency may occur. The first response is to position you and your vehicle away from oncoming traffic. Once you are off the road safely, remain in your vehicle with the doors locked and windows rolled up. This prevents someone from putting their hands through the window to open the door to reach you. Use your cell phone to call for assistance from a friend, family member, auto club, towing company or the police. When a cell phone is not available, find a nearby emergency phone.

Guide 7: Park your vehicle in an area that is open, populated and well lit. Avoid dark, isolated areas, isolated buildings, and parking spots near wooded or thick shrubbery areas.

Guide 8: Park safely. Visually scan the entire area before you approach the parking lot and continue to be observant as you approach your vehicle. Have your keys in your hand so you can get in your vehicle quickly, if needed. *Always be aware of who and what is around you.* Some predators conceal themselves by lying underneath a vehicle, waiting.

Guide 9: When exiting your vehicle, lock the doors and activate the alarm system.

Guide 10: Avoid being forced into greater danger. *Never get into a stranger's vehicle or leave with a stranger.* If someone tries to force you to go with him or her, your best chance to get away is before getting into the vehicle or being dragged to a desolate area. Whatever you do, NEVER give up. Survival stories that illustrate the concept of "never giving up" are found in Chapter Eight.

Spring Break

Parties, girls, boys, and "fun-in-the-sun." This is the time for you to take a break from the demands and stress of college life. Go and have fun with your friends and intermingle with the other hundreds to thousands of college students doing the same thing. You deserve it!

The Safety Smart Spring Break Plan for you is to arrive to your spring break destination safely, have fun, and return to college safely. Spring break requires you to have a heightened sense of awareness for your personal safety. Key safety considerations are presented to help you have a happier and safer spring break.

15 Spring Break Safety Guides:

Guide 1: Tell your parents ahead of time about your spring break plans. Tell them where you are going and who you will be with. Give them the name of the hotel, condo, or other accommodations where you will be staying. Give them a phone number where you can be reached, in addition to them having your cellular phone number.

Guide 2: Secure your valuables and financial papers in your home so others cannot get access to your personal things while you are away. You will want to store your bicycle in your room or apartment. Bike thieves love to "shop and steal" while you are away on spring break. Thieves know your college schedule. Remember, you want to be a step ahead of the criminal.

Guide 3: Do not advertise to the lurking criminal that you are away on spring break. To avoid having newspapers and subscription magazines piling up near your doorway; either temporarily cancel the subscriptions or have a neighbor or friend come by and pick them up for you.

Guide 4: Plan your travel ahead of time. Have your cellular phone and charger with you, a travel map, flashlight, a good spare tire, and an emergency car kit with you when you travel.

Guide 5: Have your vehicle checked; to include the battery, tires, fluids, and also have an oil change when your vehicle has not been maintained for quite some time.

Guide 6: When driving your vehicle, drive safely. The anticipation and excitement of spring break can distract you from paying close enough attention to the road and your driving. You want to get yourself and your friends to your destination safely. Accidents happen instantaneously.

Guide 7: When you reach your destination, make sure your vehicle trunk is closed and doors and windows are locked as you carry your luggage to your room. *Lock your car.*

Guide 8: Predators are fully aware of what goes on during spring break and astutely aware that many students will let their guard down during this time. It is a good time for you, once again, to frustrate the predator because you are smarter than he or she is, by not allowing the opportunity to exist.

Guide 9: Spring break includes alcohol consumption. This is the way it is, so what is necessary to remember is not to overindulge by drinking too much where you do not know what you are doing, and the next day, do not remember what you did. This state of mind does make you extremely vulnerable to accidents, injury, predator intrusion, and even death.

Guide 10: The primary focus here is for men. Be careful not to hang over a balcony and end up falling to your death. During spring break, this tragedy is becoming a prevalent occurrence. Do not let it happen to you. Be conscientious not to be reckless with yourself. *You are not infallible.*

Guide 11: Drug use during spring break - S*tay away from it!*

Guide 12: You and your friends have to look after one another to ensure your safety and theirs during spring break. *Go out together and come home together should always be your motto.* Under no circumstance should you ever get into a vehicle with someone you do not know. It is also not safe to give someone a ride that you do not know. Dangerous predators know how to fit in with the college crowd, and you will think this potentially dangerous person is just another student. The college women that fell victim to Ted Bundy did not feel unsafe with him, and trusted being alone with him. They never knew that they were in the hands of one of the most heinous serial killers.

Guide 13: Many students will drink too much on spring break. In a situation when you have a friend that has drank an absorbent amount of alcohol to the point that his or her life is in danger, call an ambulance and make sure your friend gets immediate medical attention. So many lives could have been saved if this had been done in these situations. You can also be personally liable if you do nothing.

Guide 14: While on spring break, you will go out to many clubs, and group activities. When you are out, no matter what you are drinking, never leave your drink unattended where someone can slip you a drug in your drink. Spring break is a time when you are even more susceptible for this to happen to you. Do not think that it will not happen to you. *It can!* Rapist will most often target women, but men, although this is not a common occurrence for you, you are not excluded. *It can happen!*

Guide 15: Since spring break also breaks out the booze, do not drink and drive and do not become a passenger with a drunk driver. When spring break is over, and you travel back to college, you want to return safely with happy memories, not a tragic one.

Chapter 5
PROPERTY CRIME, ROBBERY & BOMB THREATS

Ask Yourself: How easy is it to steal from me?

Property crime is the leading type of crime for both college campuses and communities throughout the United Sates. How widespread is it? According to the 1999 FBI Uniform Crime Report (UCR), figures for that year show stolen property is estimated to have a monetary value of 14.8 billion dollars. Crime reports for 1999 reflect a decrease in property crime since 1978, however property crime still remains an ongoing and widespread problem for U. S. colleges and communities.

What age group experiences greater incidents of victimization from property crime? If you guessed college age, you are right. According to the Office of Juvenile Justice and Delinquency Prevention, 18 to 24 year olds are the age group most susceptible to victimization of property crimes.

What is property crime? Property crime categories include theft, burglary, and arson. The FBI's UCR defines property crime as "...the offenses of burglary, larceny-theft, motor vehicle theft, and arson." "The object of the theft type offenses is the taking of money or property, but there is no force against the victim. Arson is included since it involves the destruction of property; its victims may be subjected to force."

THEFT: The Number One Property Crime

The FBI's UCR Theft definition is "the unlawful taking, carrying, leading, or riding away of property from the possession or constructive possession of another. Examples are thefts of bicycles or automobile accessories, shoplifting, pocket picking, or the stealing of any property or article, which is not taken by force and violence or by fraud. Attempted larcenies are included."

Practical scenarios are presented below to illustrate common property crimes that are perpetrated against college students. Safety guides follow each exercise.

Theft Scenario Exercise

Visualize yourself at the college library studying for an upcoming final exam. It is quiet and the people around you appear to be other students doing the same thing you are doing: studying. Needing extra information, you walk away from the table you are sitting at to use a nearby computer. Under the table is your backpack with contents that include your wallet, house and car keys. Moments after, you return to the table and continue studying. When it is time to leave, you notice your backpack is gone. You immediately look around but have no idea where it went or who has taken it. The thief or thieves now have your wallet, your personal identification, keys to your car and house, and those expensive textbooks that you do not have money to replace. You are bewildered and think, "I only left for a minute." You start to panic, and then decide to call the campus police to report the theft. The officer arrives to take a theft report from you and you begin to tell the officer what happened.

What can you expect at this point? The officer will ask you a series of questions designed to help him or her identify and apprehend the thief or thieves and have your property returned to you. The following are some of the questions you will be asked: When was the last time you had your backpack? What was in the backpack? When did you realize the backpack was missing? What does your backpack look like? Where did you put your backpack? Did you see anyone near your table? Unless there was a witness to the theft or a video surveillance camera captured the theft in progress and the thief can be identified, the officer's chances of catching the thief and returning your property are not promising.

Theft Scenario Review

Thieves are consistently on the lookout for an opportunity to steal. The theft is usually pre-planned and many times the thief plans more than one theft for that given time and place. In this scenario, numerous thefts were planned at the library that day, so our victim was one of several. Thieves are clever, sneaky and greedy. One theft is never enough. These thefts could have been prevented.

An analysis of this scenario reveals a lot of potential to prevent the theft from ever occurring. Before you go into the library, decide what you really need to have with you. If you drive your car to the library, you can secure the items you do not need in a locked trunk or locked glove compartment. Then lock your car and activate your car alarm. Do not put keys in your backpack; they can easily fit in the front pocket of your pants. Bring only the textbooks you need and keep your belongings with you at all times. When you have to leave your table for any reason, take your backpack and textbooks with you. Although this is inconvenient, it is more inconvenient to have your property stolen from you. These safety guides significantly reduce opportunities for thieves to steal from you.

Property Identification Programs

Campus and city police departments, and the sheriff's office offer property identification programs that are designed to document your valuable property. Your property's identifying information, such as, the serial numbers is tied to a decal number that is assigned to the property item. Bicycles are an excellent example of the value of this program. One of the biggest problems on college campuses are stolen bicycles. U-locks are a must to lock your bicycle, but it is not a fail-safe device for the thief. Bike thieves will challenge and conquer many locking devices, to steal your bicycle. Register your bicycle with the campus police or city police or sheriff's department to make sure you have a record of your bicycle's identifying information just in case your bicycle is stolen. Without identifying information to affiliate the bicycle to you as the legal owner, how do you prove that the bicycle is, in fact, yours.

The Right Way

The Wrong Way

Preventing theft involves the following seven safety guides.

7 Theft Prevention Safety Smart Guides

Guide 1: Secure your property at all times, to include having a record kept that documents the serial numbers of your property. Take advantage of the property identification programs offered by law enforcement agencies in your community.

Guide 2: Use locking devices that are difficult to break and are hard to open without a key, such as a U-lock.

Guide 3: Avoid leaving property unattended.

Guide 4: The less you carry, the less to steal.

Guide 5: Be aware of who is around you.

Guide 6: Be suspicious of people who do not look like they belong.

Guide 7: Report suspicious persons and incidents to police.

BURGLARY: Entering a Structure to Steal or Commit a Felony

The FBI's UCR definition for burglary is, "breaking or entering - the unlawful entry of a structure to commit a felony or a theft. Attempted forcible entry is included." According to FBI statistics, a residential burglary occurs every 15 seconds. According to the U. S. Department of Education, the on-campus burglary rate is 156 per 100,000 enrolled students. The following information shows that 4-year public colleges have experienced a decline in burglary incidents, whereas 4-year private colleges are experiencing an increase in burglary.

Burglary On-Campus	1997	1998	1999
Public	16,642	15,748	15,173
Private, non-profit	9,488	9,167	9,772
Private, for-profit	627	770	1,090

(Source: U. S. Department of Education, Office of Postsecondary Education, Report to Congress, 2001)

The following scenario provides an example of a burglary incident on a college campus.

Burglary Scenario Exercise

It is your second year in college and you and two roommates share a campus apartment. On Saturday, your roommates are out shopping and you have the apartment to yourself. Feeling secure in your surroundings, you do not bother to lock your apartment door when you decide to visit two friends at a nearby apartment. An hour goes by and you return to your apartment. Nothing looks out of the ordinary and you do not suspect that anyone has gone into your apartment to steal anything. You decide to meet your roommates at the shopping mall, and go to get your wallet that you left on the kitchen counter. The wallet's contents included your weekly spending money, credit cards, driver license, and student ID. The wallet is gone.

Once you realize someone has entered your home and stolen your property, phone the campus or local police department. Since the intruder may still be in your apartment or building, think of your safety first. Go to a safe place and call the police. The questions you will be asked by the police officer are similar to those in scenario one: who, what, where, and when. Where was your wallet? What does your wallet look like? When was the last time you had your wallet? What time did you realize the wallet was missing? Who else has access to your apartment other than you and your roommates? Where were you at the time? Where were your roommates at the time? Was the door locked or unlocked? Were your windows locked or open? The questions continue until the officer has enough information to try to find the person who entered your apartment and committed burglary.

Burglary Scenario Review

Lock your door and keep your property in a secure place in your apartment and/or room. An unlocked door lets an intruder, in this case a burglar, enter your home to commit a crime. This situation can worsen, and becomes more unpredictable when perpetrators decide to wait for you and/or your roommates to return home, in order to rape or commit other violent crimes. Did you know that before Ted Bundy and Danny Rolling committed rape and murder, they both were known to commit theft and burglary? Locking doors, even when you plan to leave for only a minute, and locking your windows, deters crime from happening. As in all other crimes, it is important to remember to avoid destroying evidence after a burglary. The police may be able to lift fingerprints, so it is important that you and your roommates avoid touching anything. Provide the police officer with information about the property taken, such as the value of the property, model numbers, serial numbers, and descriptions of the stolen property. Nine safety guides for preventing burglary follow.

9 Burglary Prevention Safety Smart Guides

Guide 1: Keep your doors and windows locked.

Guide 2: When you go out for the evening, leave a light on in your residence, and also the outside entrance lights, including those for the garage or side entrances.

Guide 3: Do not let newspapers, magazines and mail gather around your entranceway and mailbox. These visible indicators say, "I'm not home."

Guide 4: Lawns and shrubbery need to be trimmed for visibility and openness.

Guide 5: Home alarm systems enhance your security. Newer apartment complexes usually have security alarms, and for those residences without a system, consider installing one.

Guide 6: Keys left in a flowerpot, under a mat, or similar hiding places make your home into an easy target.

Guide 7: Join a neighborhood crime watch program and report suspicious persons and activities to the police.

Guide 8: Request a residential security inspection of your home.

Guide 9: Never leave valuables in plain view for others to see and steal.

ARSON: Dangerous and Life-threatening Fires

Arson, the intentional starting of fires, is a serious public safety threat. The death of Michael Minger, in 1998, is an example of a tragic death of a college student. His death was because of an arson fire in his residence hall. In March 2000, Kentucky Governor Paul Patton signed The Michael Minger Act into law. This Act mandates that colleges licensed by the Kentucky Council on Postsecondary Education maintain public crime logs reporting campus crimes to students, employees and the public. This Act stipulates that colleges in the State of Kentucky must report threats of fire and arson incidents to the State Fire Marshall and other officials, and also gives the State Fire Marshall access to college property to inspect, investigate and prevent fire loss. This includes determining the origin of fires.

Figures from the U. S. Department of Education's Report to Congress for the year 1999 show the total number of arsons that occurred on campus property reached 1167. For the same year, in residence halls, there were 623 incidents of arson. Non-campus arson incidents totaled 147 and arson incidents on public property totaled 538. From this data, it is clear that arson fires are considerably higher on campus property than on non-campus property. Arson fires are a severe threat to life and property.

The FBI's UCR definition for arson is, "Any willful or malicious burning or attempt to burn, with or without intent to defraud, a dwelling house, public building, motor vehicle or aircraft, personal property of another, etc."

Arson Scenario Exercise

You live in a student residential complex on campus. You observe another student setting a fire in a trashcan in the building's hallway. You do not want to be a snitch, so you do not say anything, and thinking the fire is out, you leave. But it is not. Later, you hear that the fire destroyed the section of the building where the fire was initially ignited.

Arson Scenario Review

Practical jokes such as setting a fire in a trashcan is dangerous and can be life-threatening to all the residents that live in the building. The crime of arson involves serious criminal penalties, this is also in violation of college regulations. For non-arson related incidents, Chapter Three covers fire safety and responding to a fire alarm in residential areas. Seven safety guides to prevent arson are presented below.

7 Arson Prevention Safety Smart Guides

Guide 1: Report fire or a burning odor immediately by calling 911.

Guide 2: Pranksters that set fires should be reported to authorities.

Guide 3: Follow the rules and regulations involving fire safety.

Guide 4: Know the locations of fire extinguishers and fire alarms.

Guide 5: Tampering with or damaging fire equipment is a serious crime and the penalties are serious.

Guide 6: Immediately report damaged and missing fire extinguishers or smoke detectors to housing officials or landlords.

Guide 7: Smokers: use designated smoking areas.

Motor Vehicle Theft

The Department of Education's Report to Congress shows that in 1999, 6201 motor vehicle thefts occurred on U.S. college campuses. We need to better protect our vehicles from criminal opportunists both on-campus and off-campus. An automobile is one of the most valuable and important possessions you have. Your ability to protect yourself while you are operating your vehicle, and how well you protect your vehicle, can minimize the probability of your vehicle being stolen. Having your car stolen not only takes away your method of transportation, but the related economic considerations affect you and everyone else with a motor vehicle. Insurance premiums increase. Also, your stolen car may become involved in a crash, contributing to further economic loss. Factors that influence motor vehicle theft include geography and vehicle popularity.

What type of vehicles do thieves prefer stealing? Thieves target vehicles that offer the best possible market for stolen parts or exportation. Geographic factors also influence what vehicles are popular targets for motor vehicle theft. For example, in Austin, Texas, the pickup truck may be the criminal choice, whereas in Albany, New York, the Honda Accord may be chosen. In 1999, the National Insurance Crime Bureau, Florida Auto Theft Intelligence Unit conducted a study and identified the ten most commonly stolen vehicles: the Honda Accord, Toyota Camry, Oldsmobile Cutlass, Chevrolet full size pickup, Honda Civic, Toyota Corolla, Jeep Cherokee, Chevrolet Caprice, Ford Taurus and Chevrolet Cavalier.

Safety Smart Ways to Prevent Motor Vehicle Theft

Several preventative measures decrease the chance that your automobile will be stolen. Advanced technology contributes to auto-theft prevention. Most late model vehicles have a theft-deterrent device installed by the manufacturer. Most insurance companies give the insurer a discount for having an auto theft alarm. According to the 1999 Highway Loss Data Institute (HLDI) Study, significantly fewer theft claims were filed for 1999 cars with a factory-installed anti-theft device compared to 1998 automobiles without an anti-theft device.

SSS Web reference: More information about anti-theft and insurance issues can be found at web site http://www.insure.com.

Anti-theft devices prevent auto thefts. Although many college students do not drive late model cars with factory installed anti-theft devices, they still need alternative methods to protect their vehicle. A couple methods are to make sure you lock your doors at all times and have an auto theft alarm installed. For those who want to upgrade their vehicle with an anti-theft device, visit your local or campus police to inquire about possible options. Some alarm systems available are fuel shut-off devices, ignition cut-off armored devices and locking devices for vehicle hoods. One of the best basic deterrents is to lock your vehicle's door and keep the windows rolled up.

In many auto theft cases, the driver of the vehicle left the keys in the ignition or somewhere in the car. A thief will check under your seat and in your glove compartment for keys. Both joy riders and professional thieves look for autos that are the easiest to steal. Joy riders are usually teenagers who steal cars spontaneously. They steal a car, take it for a ride and dump it somewhere else later. The professional auto thief plans the crime. They may want the auto to commit another crime, for chop-shop distribution (that is, to sell it for parts) or for resale. Leaving your keys in the car, leaving windows rolled down, parking in isolated and dark areas, all contribute to allowing an auto thief to steal your vehicle. Auto theft can occur anytime of the day or night, but thieves prefer the evening hours. Popular places auto thieves seek out opportunities include large parking lots, shopping malls, airport terminals and parking areas where events are drawing a large crowd, such as stadiums. During events that draw crowds, avoid parking your vehicle in an isolated area, and be particularly vigilant about locking your vehicle and rolling up the windows. During large events such as football games, the police department will increase their patrols of parking lots and parking garages.

Keep Your Valuables Out-of-Sight

Leaving valuable items in plain view and unsecured in your car provokes theft and burglary. The trunk of your vehicle is the best place to store valuables. A criminal will check your glove compartment, as well as the back and front seat areas. Wallets, money, cameras, CD players left in plain view encourage thieves. Always think in terms of denying opportunities to criminals.

IDENTITY THEFT
The Criminal Is Now Stealing Your Identity

Criminals are becoming more sophisticated in their criminal behavior and shrewder in selecting their targets. Identity theft is increasing and is potentially dangerous because the thief is able to learn a great deal about you in addition to hurting you financially. The criminal has found many ways to do this: stealing your wallet, obtaining personal information from the Internet, acquiring your credit report, intercepting personal mail, and even going through your trash to retrieve personal papers. A thief may fill out a change of address form and have your mail re-routed to a post office box, or other bogus location. In that case, your new credit cards, or loan papers are sent directly to the thief without your knowledge. This gives him or her the ability to use your identify to acquire credit cards, bank accounts, loans or other services in your name. The nightmare begins as your credit line dissipates, your credit is ruined, and a high debt is now pointed at you because your personal identify has been fraudulently used by a resourceful, smart thief.

Becoming a victim of identify theft can crush your ability to conduct your daily college activities in a positive and effective way.

Once the thief has gathered personal information about you, such as your name, address, phone number, date of birth, account numbers and social security number, the thief can use your identify. In today's society, you cannot leave your personal property or personal information unsecured even for a minute. Many student victims of theft say, "I only left for a minute, and when I returned my backpack, wallet, money, books, or keys were gone. I did not see anyone take my property." Thieves watch their targets and their surroundings for the right opportunity to commit a crime. Your safety smartness involves always securing your personal identifying information, and retaining possession of your property. Deterring identify theft requires a higher level of personal awareness. Keep your personal information confidential and protected from others.

When you have to fill out financial, college or work applications that require personal information, such as a social security number, ask who else has access to this information and who is this information shared with. Student information pertaining to education records is protected under the Family Education Rights and Privacy Act (FERPA), also known as the "Buckley Amendment." This Act provides you with certain privacy rights whereby the college cannot release your information to a third party without your permission. Exemptions to this amendment include parents of students that are under 18 years of age, school officials employed or contracted with by the college, and the College Board of Trustees. College officials must have a "need to know" for official reasons to access student information. The Buckley Amendment also provides you with access to your educational records. Designated college officials or the dean of students can provide you with additional information about this Act, and answer questions you may have about securing the privacy of your personal information.

Other Loopholes to Steal Your Identify

The mailbox is another target for the criminal. Mailboxes should be secured with a locking device and not shared with others. I highly recommend that you obtain a private mailbox or post office box.

How do you dispose of your mail and other personal papers? When cleaning your files of old or replicated bills, statements, expired credit cards and other documents that provide an array of personal data and account information, shred these personal papers. You can purchase inexpensive shredders at office supply stores and discount stores for under $20. Cut up old credit cards before putting them into the trash, since identity thieves even go so far as rummaging through trash to find personal identifying information.

Other security methods include the use of passwords to protect your accounts. It is not uncommon for people to use their date of birth or a family member's name as a password. It is best, however, to create a password that is not personally related to you. Once you have established your password, refrain from giving it to others, or writing it down for others to see, since that is counterproductive to securing personal property. Be aware that the college's telephone directory lists your residence and phone number and is assessable to the public, unless you specifically request that this information not be disclosed. If you wish to have your personal directory information restricted from disclosure in the college's hard-copy directory book, or on the college's web site directory listings, you must request this from the college registrar. There will be a written form you will be required to complete.

SSS **W**eb reference: http://www.asu.edu/counsel/brief/ferpa/html provides additional information about student educational records.

SSS **W**eb reference: More information about identity theft can be found at, http://www.ftc.gov/bcp/conline/pubs/credit/idtheft.html.

Knowing what personal information a thief is likely to seek can help you stay one step ahead of them. The following list gives the information thieves would like to know about you:

* Your name and date of birth
* Social security number
* Bank account numbers
* Credit card numbers
* Income
* Home/work address and phone number
* Name of your college

> * Your workplace
> * Where you bank

The following safety guides will help protect you from identity theft.

7 Safety Smart Guides to Protect Your Identity

Guide 1: Do not give other people, other than for legitimate, official purposes, your personal information, including phone numbers, social security number, date of birth, parent's name, your financial institution, account numbers, income and income source (federal loans, bank loans). Your password protect codes should not be shared with anyone.

Guide 2: Most college students have roommates, acquaintances and friends coming into their rooms or apartments. Put your personal papers and cards where others cannot see or take them. Personal papers and cards include bank statements, college records, financial aid information, car insurance records, credit card receipts and statements. Do not let anyone have access to your credit cards, bank cards, college ID cards, driver's license, social security card, and checkbooks. Secure these items in a safe place.

Guide 3: Have your own private mailbox and keep your key secure from others.

Guide 4: When you provide personal identification numbers on forms for college admission, financial institutions, college and work applications, ask how the information is secured, who has access to this information, and who is this information shared with.

Guide 5: Use a shredder to shred personal papers you want to discard.

Guide 6: Refrain from telling others anything about your financial status.

Guide 7: Your social security number connects you with just about every transaction you carry out. When you provide your social security number, make sure it is necessary to do so. For example, if a retail business asks you for your social security when you issue a personal check for merchandise, instead of providing your social security number, provide your driver's license number when a business wants identification for personal checks.

Credit cards can get you into trouble, not only by accumulating a large balance with an astronomical interest rate, but thieves are notorious for stealing credit cards. When you receive your credit card in the mail, immediately sign the back of the card. Many credit cards have your photo on the face of the card, making it harder for the theft to use your credit card. It is also important to retain all your credit card receipts and every month check these receipts with your monthly bill. Your credit card should never be given to a roommate or friend to use. In situations when your credit card is lost, stolen or missing, immediately report it to your credit card company, and write down and retain the confirmation number they give you. Also, when you use the Internet to subscribe to on-line services, refrain from giving out your password and credit card number. When you do purchase merchandise from the Internet, make sure your credit card information is protected.

How You Can Stop Telephone, Mail and Email Solicitation

Some people, including established businesses, will readily sell your personal information to telephone, mail and email solicitors. You are then vulnerable to both identity theft and harassment from solicitors. The following information will help you end unwanted solicitation and deter fraudulent activity. The Direct Marketing Association (DMA) is an organization that helps consumers have their name removed from marketing lists that are commonly given to direct marketing organizations. To have your name removed from direct mail lists, write to: DMA Mail Preference Service, P.O. Box 9008, Farmingdale, NY 11735-9008. To have your name removed from direct phone lists, the address to write is: DMA Telephone Preference Service, P. O. Box 9014, Farmingdale, NY 11735-9014. To remove your name from direct email lists, go to: http://www.e-mps.org. This may not keep all direct marketers from contacting you by phone, mail, or email, but it should significantly reduce unwanted solicitation.

How You Can Avoid Victimization from ID Theft or Fraud

Report ID theft or fraud to the police department having jurisdiction where the crime occurred. For example, if you live on campus and the theft occurred at your residence or other campus property areas, contact the campus police department. Otherwise, contact either the city police or sheriff's office, depending on the jurisdiction where the crime occurred. Make sure you get a copy of the police report for your records and forward a copy to the credit card companies involved.

In addition to reporting ID theft or fraud to the police, three primary credit bureau agencies - Equifax, Experian, and Trans Union - need to be contacted. Equifax address is, P.O. Box 105873, Atlanta, GA 30348-5873. Their telephone number is 1-800-997-2493. Experian Information Solutions address is, P.O. Box 949, Allen, TX 75013-0949. Their telephone number is 1-888-397-3742. The TransUnion address is, P.O. Box 390, Springfield, PA 19064-0390. Their telephone number is 1-800-916-8800. This information is also provided in Chapter 16.

The U.S. Postal Inspection Service suggest you report identity theft to the three credit bureau agencies provided and also the Federal Trade Commission, local police, U.S. Postal Inspection Service and U.S. Postal Service, and Social Security Administration Fraud Hotline at 1-800-269-0271.

SSS Web reference: For more information about the U.S. Postal Inspections Service	http://www.usps.gov/postalinspectors

SSS Web reference: For more information on ID Theft or credit card fraud go to: http://www.ftc.gov/bcp/conline/pubs/credit/idtheft.htm.

This web site will also provide you with sample dispute letters to credit bureaus and tell you how to contact these credit bureaus and report identify theft to stop future illegal and fraudulent credit-related activities. Your financial credit rating and further victimization is at risk if you become a victim of identity theft. Contact creditors that issued you the credit cards. Back up the call with a written letter stating the name of the company representative you spoke with and the date and time of the call. Further resolution of credit problems may be necessary. The Fair Credit Reporting Act (FCRA) addresses disputes about errors on credit reports. Another act to know about is The Truth in Lending Act. This act limits the liability that individuals can incur because of unauthorized use of their credit cards. The liability limit for each card is usually set at $50. The Fair Debt Collection Practices Act addresses the problem of creditors who use unfair practices in collecting overdue payments. The Electronic Fund Transfer Act is a protection act that pertains to your ATM card, debit card or other electronic transfer methods. This act sets a limit to individual liability because of illegal and unauthorized transfer activities. Immediately report lost or stolen ATM or debit cards to the financial institution that issued the card. Potential financial loss can escalate when a person delays notifying their card providers. For example, if a lost or stolen ATM card if reported within two business days of when the card was lost or stolen, personal liability is limited to $50. If notification is delayed more than two business days, personal liability can escalate to $500. Always follow up a phone call with a written letter to make sure your notification was documented. Be smart about all your financial dealings. Protect your identity, the quality of your life, and your future financial security.

ROBBERY: The Use of Force to Steal from You

Robbery is not considered a property crime because force or the threat of force is an element of this crime. Robbery is, "the taking or attempting to take anything of value from the care, custody, or control of a person or persons by force or threat of force or violence and/or by putting the victim in fear."

According to the Department of Education, 12 out of every 100,000 college students were victimized by on-campus robberies in 1999. The chart below gives the number of incidences of on-campus robberies for public and private colleges for the years 1997, 1998, and

1999. From this data, you can see that robberies have decreased at public institutions, and increased for private non-profit and for-profit institutions.

Robberies On-Campus			
	1997	1998	1999
Public	1133	1084	1005
Private, non-profit	565	639	733
Private, for-profit	112	139	259

Department of Education, Office of Postsecondary Education, A Report to Congress, January 2001.

The following scenario will help you avoid becoming the victim of a robbery and help you deal with the situation if you are robbed. You're walking to chemistry class early one morning, and because you are running a little late, you decide to take a short cut along a wooded pathway not often used by students. The path is isolated and cannot be easily seen from the sidewalk or roadway. As you are rushing to class along this path, two men approach you and demand your wallet. You freeze as one of the men forcibly pushes you to the ground and grabs your backpack. Then both men run away. You are now going to be late for class, or miss it completely, and you are a victim of robbery.

Being robbed is frightening and dangerous. Robbers may use a weapon during a robbery. Your first priority is to get away from the danger and find a safe place. Once you find a safe place, contact the police. The sooner you report the robbery, the better chance the officers have to apprehend those who robbed you. The officer will ask you if you are hurt and need medical attention. If you have been injured, get medical care. Immediate medical attention takes precedence over an investigation. Provide the police officer with a description of the person(s) who robbed you: race, height, weight, eye color, facial hair, clothing, tattoos, etc. You will also need to answer the "W" questions previously mentioned. What were the robbers wearing, (blue baseball cap, gold jewelry, blue short-sleeve shirt, etc.)? What direction did they flee? When did the robbery occur? Where did the robbery occur? Did anyone witness the robbery? What happened? Have you ever seen the perpetrators before? Did they get into a vehicle (if so, describe the vehicle)?

In any robbery situation, your life is always more important than any money or property you own. Give up your wallet without a fight. Chances are you will not win the fight and you can get seriously injured or killed. Your wallet can be replaced; you cannot! The following safety guides will help you avoid becoming the victim of a robbery.

4 Safety Smart Robbery Prevention Guides

Guide 1: Avoid the off-the-beaten-track paths that isolate you.

Guide 2: Be attentive to who and what is around you.

Guide 3: Avoid flaunting or exposing your money or other valuables.

Guide 4: Report suspicious persons and activities to the police.

BOMB THREATS

We all remember that on Tuesday, September 11, 2001, terrorist attacks on America resulted in catastrophic and heartbreaking loss of human life and American property. The destruction of the World Trade Center's twin towers in New York City and part of the Pentagon in Washington D.C. are terrorist acts that remain freshly imprinted in the minds of the American people. We now realize that our lives and our property are vulnerable to personal attack. A heightened sense of awareness is paramount for your personal safety and the safety of others.

Before enrolling at the college of your choice, obtain information from the campus crime prevention division about bomb threats on college campuses. A college campus is not exempt or sheltered from terrorist cell activities and bomb threats. Most bomb threats on college campuses are initiated by college students and disgruntled employees. Bomb threats adversely impact students' academic performance and their desire to remain in college. How do bomb threats affect students academically? Students, faculty and staff who are evacuated from a building because of a bomb threat do experience fear, anger and frustration. Students have expressed experiencing these emotions and some students have either withdrawn from the class in the threatened building or have left college entirely because they do not feel safe after a bomb threat. Making bomb threats is a serious crime and the punishment is severe. Threatening to plant a bomb, making false reports about planting bombs or explosives, planting a fake bomb, or planting a real bomb are all felony crimes.

Why do some college students make bomb threats? Reasons include, a way to get out of class or a scheduled examination, frustration with a class instructor or with the college as a whole. Students who call in bogus bomb threats because they want to create a diversion may not understand the seriousness of this crime. Understand that the legal repercussions of making bomb threats or carrying out any activities related to explosives are severe.

A Warning to EVACUATE

College students, who may either ignore the warning or leave the building and then stand right next to it, do not always take bomb threats on a college campus seriously. It is dangerous to assume that the bomb threat is a hoax. At the time the evacuation is initiated, authorities do not know whether a bomb has been planted or not. To maximize your personal safety, leave the building calmly and distance yourself at least 300 feet from the building or targeted area. Abide by the designated perimeters set by police or fire officials. Your local police and fire departments are an excellent source of further information about bomb threats and protective methods.

Taking the Bomb Threat Call

This is one time you do not want to hang up the phone, as you would with an obscene or harassing phone call. Now you are the one who needs to ask the "W" questions. Calmly ask the following questions: Where is the bomb? When is the bomb going to explode? What does the bomb look like? Why is the bomb planted? Who planted the bomb? Listen to background noises, since that may help police determine where the call was placed. Pay attention to the caller. Is the person male or female? Does he/she sound old or young? Does he/she have an accent? Write down verbatim what the caller is saying. Your life and the lives of many others may depend on what the caller is saying. Any instructions given by the caller may be especially critical to the safety of all involved. Notify the police immediately. If possible, have a nearby person call the police while you talk to the caller. The longer you are able to keep the caller on the phone, the better chance the police will have of detecting the location of the caller. Give all the information you obtain from the caller to police officials.

Any time you observe suspicious persons or activities, or have information about any threatening acts or behaviors, contact the police immediately.

Chapter 6
AUTOMATIC TELLER MACHINES & BANK CARD FRAUD

Ask Yourself: Do I use ATM's that are located in safe places?

It is Saturday evening at 10:00 P.M. and a few of your friends want you to join them at a popular club downtown. You need to stop at a nearby automatic teller machine (ATM) and pick up some extra cash for the evening. Seems safe enough, right? Most times yes, but not necessarily always. The ATM has made it convenient for us to easily access money any time of the day or night. This convenience and easy access to our personal accounts also generates opportunities for criminals. The criminal's adrenaline accelerates while he or she watches an ATM transaction because the criminal's goal is to take away your money as soon as you get it. When your attention is on getting money from the ATM and meeting friends, you may not be paying attention to who and what is around. Your inattention is what the criminal is depending on.

The criminal may decide to go a step further and physically harm you. With this in mind, it is helpful to review safety smart practices to enhance self-protection when using an ATM. Whenever possible use the ATM during daytime hours when other people are around. Use an ATM that is in an open and lighted area. The criminal is less inclined to approach you when there are people all around, or in a well-lit area. The choices you make can close the door of opportunity for anyone to steal from you or cause you physical harm. Choosing a safe and protected situation for yourself makes you smarter than the criminal.

Colleen Kenniston

Assess the safety of an ATM's physical location before deciding to use it. You want to avoid using ATM's located in a dark corner of a building where shrubbery and trees hinder visibility. Many banks have an ATM located outside the drive-through teller area, to give their customers easy accessibility to the ATM. Although this location is convenient, it may not be safe when the bank's drive-through teller is closed. The ATM does not close when the drive-through teller windows close, so that changes safety factors. Another important factor is where the drive-through teller area is physically located. Often, the drive-through teller window is located on the side or back of the building. This may be a place of isolation, reduced visibility, and dim lighting, conditions that favor the criminal, not you. The criminal can now approach you on foot or in a vehicle. Using a drive-through ATM is safer during business hours when the drive-through is open, and not as safe after hours when the drive-through teller is closed. Most ATM's are equipped with video cameras for monitoring purposes. Video cameras are an effective crime prevention tool. However, the most effective preventive tool is you and your personal safety smartness.

CAMPUS ATM's

As a new student on an unfamiliar college campus, find out where the ATM's are located. Use an ATM that offers the best safety factors, as discussed above. Most college campuses have several ATM's located at the student union building and other densely populated areas. These are the best places to conduct an ATM transaction, when the building is open and busy with student, faculty and staff activities. Reassess the same location to determine the safety factors during the evening and late night hours. Avoid areas that are dark and isolated at night, and do not use that ATM after hours.

After you have identified safe ATM locations, there are additional considerations to keep in mind when using an ATM. Again, be aware of your surroundings and notice suspicious activity or people around you. Reporting such activities or persons to the nearest police department, involves becoming familiar with the college's emergency phone locations. If you observe suspicious activity or persons while conducting your ATM transaction, it is best to terminate the transaction immediately and leave. You can always use another ATM elsewhere.

Using your instincts and intuition enhances your ability to recognize suspicious activity and people. None of us like the feeling of someone standing too close to us when we are using an ATM. It gives us an uneasy feeling and rightfully so. Maybe the person is just being inconsiderate or is not aware of crowding you while you use the ATM. Maybe he or she is trying to observe the pin number you enter into the ATM, or find out how much money you are getting out of the machine. When money is extracted from the machine, the first thing we want to do is count it. A criminal opportunist will watch avidly while you count your money in plain view. Do not do it.

Your ATM card enables you to access your accounts. By giving someone your pin number, or writing it in your checkbook, on your ATM cardholder, or any place where another person can see it, you have created an opportunity for other people to access your accounts. A criminal can clean out your account before you even know you have lost control of your pin number. Incident reports show that college students become victims when their pin numbers are given to someone or found by a thief. A thief isn't always a stranger. He or she can be a friend or roommate. The practice of writing a pin number down on a piece of paper and leaving it out in an apartment or dorm room where friends, acquaintances and roommates can see it, presents the opportunity for one of these people to steal from you. Your bank or debit card is no longer secure if anyone obtains the card's pin number.

After completing an ATM transaction, people have a tendency to throw their transaction receipt either on the ground or in a nearby trashcan. This presents opportunity where a criminal can pick it up, read it to find out information about you, including how much money is in your account. This tells a criminal how much money they can steal. The best practice is to keep the receipts and statements in a locked file at home, or shred and dispose of transaction documents at home.

The Criminal is Always Thinking of Ways to Steal

The criminal has other clever ways to obtain information about you and your financial accounts. Telephones and personal computers can be used to con you into giving out pertinent information about you and your accounts. A person calls you claiming to be Mr. Smith, the loan officer of your bank. Mr. Smith tells you he is conducting a customer survey and needs you to answer a few questions or he tells you that he is calling to verify that you received your ATM card. He then asks you to give him your pin number for bank purposes. Whenever a bank or credit card company calls you to request information about you or your accounts, realize the possibility that this could be a scam to steal from you. *Do not release any personal information to an unknown voice on the other end of a telephone line.* When you receive these types of calls, contact your financial institution and talk to a representative to validate the authenticity of the person calling you, and the legitimacy of the reason for calling. The same principles apply to computer scams. Seven safety guides that will better protect you when using an ATM are listed below.

7 Safety Smart Guides to Use ATM's

Guide 1: Locate and use the most open and illuminated ATM's, on and off campus.

Guide 2: Be aware that ATM's that are safe to use during the day may not be as safe at night.

Guide 3: Be aware of people and activities going on around you when using ATM's. If you see suspicious people or activities, terminate your transaction immediately. Then go to a safe place and report the suspicious people and activities to police.

Guide 4: When someone is too close to you while you are using the ATM, politely ask the person not to stand so close to you while you use the ATM. If the person does not honor your request or gives you a hard time, immediately end your transaction and leave.

Guide 5: Always discreetly count your money so others cannot easily watch you.

Guide 6: Do not throw away your ATM transaction receipts on the ground or in a nearby trashcan. Criminals will seek out your information anyway they can.

Guide 7: When using a drive-through ATM, keep your car doors locked and windows up while the transaction is processed.

Avoid dark, isolated ATM locations.

Chapter 7
OBSCENE OR HARASSING PHONE CALLS

Ask Yourself:
Do I know what to do if I receive an obscene or harassing phone call?

Obscene or harassing phone calls continue to be an ongoing problem for college students. Dormitories and apartment complexes where numerous people reside and non-residents visit contribute to security problems and the propensity for obscene and harassing phone calls. Most college students who receive these calls are females, and the caller is usually an unknown male caller, an acquaintance, or an ex-boyfriend. Male college students receive harassing and obscene phone calls less frequently. The calls can happen when a relationship ends and one of the ex-partners decides to disturb or frighten their former partner. These calls can be initiated by anyone - friends, ex-boyfriends, ex-girlfriends, acquaintances or strangers. Making verbal threats over the phone, harassing people by phone, and saying obscenities over the phone are unlawful acts. These calls are upsetting and can create fear in the person receiving the calls. Many times, the caller will make sexual comments that are indecent and abusive, causing disruption to daily activities and safety concerns.

What are Obscene or Harassing Phone Calls? Each state has its own legal definition of what constitutes an obscene or harassing telephone call. If you experience such a call, become familiar with your state's obscene or harassing phone call statute. In general terms, such calls involve indecent suggestions, profane language or threats. The caller intends to be abusive and/or threatening. Unwanted and repetitive phone calls to an individual are also considered harassing, even when the person does not say anything obscene or threatening.

An example of a state statute on Obscene or Harassing Phone Calls is Florida State Statute 365.16 which states that "(1)(a) Whoever makes a telephone call to a location at which the person receiving the call has a reasonable expectation of privacy; during such call makes any comment, request, suggestion, or proposal which is obscene, lewd, lascivious, filthy, vulgar, or indecent; and by such call or such language intends to offend, annoy, abuse, threaten, or harass any person at the called number; (b) Makes a telephone call, whether or not conversation ensues, without disclosing his or her identity and with intent to annoy, abuse, threaten, or harass any person at the called number;(c) Makes or causes the telephone of another repeatedly or continuously to ring with intent to harass any person at the called number; or (d) Makes repeated telephone calls, during which conversation ensues, solely to harass any person at the called number." (Source: F.S.S. 365.16)

Anyone who violates this state law commits a misdemeanor offense. Florida law also includes the person who lets another person use their phone for the purpose of making harassing and obscene phone calls. Some states give the victim the right to a written exemption to protect her or his identify from being disclosed. Since every state law varies, ask how your identity can be protected under state law and exercise that right.

Men: Beware of Making Prank Phone Calls

Men, this message will help you avoid being accused of making an obscene or harassing telephone call because the call was placed from your residence. How does this happen? You have friends over for a party. People you do not know end up at your party. Unbeknownst to you, some of the visitors get drunk and decide to use your phone to make obscene or harassing phone calls as a prank. A few days later you get a call from a police investigator because your phone has been identified as the phone from which the calls were placed. You are now listed as a suspect on an official police report.

Protect yourself by knowing who is in your home, what activities are happening in your home, and who is using your telephone, and for what purpose. Protect yourself and your property when people freely roam around in your home. Obscene or harassing telephone calls are not innocent pranks; they are against the law. Offenders are prosecuted through the court system and through the college judicial system as student conduct violations. Callers may think it is a joke, but they are upsetting and sometimes frightening the person receiving the call.

How You Should Handle Obscene or Harassing Phone Calls

College students frequently ask investigators, how do I stop someone from calling me and making obscene or harassing remarks? The goal is to find out who is making the calls, have the calls stopped and remain safe. To effectively accomplish this goal, tell the police everything about the caller and the calls. The more complete, articulate and detailed you are in your account, including giving the exact comments made, the more you facilitate the investigative process. Where the calls are received determines what police agency will intervene. For instance, if you receive obscene or harassing phone calls at your apartment in the city, contact the city police department. If you live outside the city limits, contact the sheriff's office. On-campus residents need to contact the campus police department to make a report.

When you receive a call and the person asks to talk to someone who does not live there, or nothing is said and the caller hangs up, this is not a harassing phone call. Tell the caller they have a wrong number. If repetitive calls are made to your phone and you hear nothing, or heavy breathing or some other disturbing sound, hang up the phone and note the date and time each call was placed. You can use the *69 feature code to find out the number of the last person who called you. A caller may activate the *60 feature code to block you from finding out the number. When you do retrieve the person's number, you may feel a strong desire to call the person back and express your displeasure personally. Do not do this. When the calls are obscene and/or harassing, it is imperative to not react in frustration or anger, nor engage yourself in any discussion with the person. This person wants you to react and the situation worsens when you try to deal with the caller personally. Write the number down and keep it in case the calls become continual and annoying and you need to contact the police.

The five safety smart guides listed will help you handle obscene or harassing phone calls.

5 Safety Smart Guides About Obscene or Harassing Telephone Calls

Guide 1: Listen, remain silent, and write down all information about the call: the time and date of the call, background noises, what was said, speech patterns, possible age and gender of the caller, etc. This does not mean to stay on the phone for any length of time. When you first realize the phone call is obscene or harassing, hang up. By doing this you are sending the caller an unspoken message that you are not going to play his or her game. Keep a log of all the obscene or harassing phone calls you receive.

Guide 2: Call the police and report the incident.

Guide 3: Get an unlisted phone number.

Guide 4: Devices such as Caller ID, *69, and function *57 (a device the phone company can use to trace calls) can be used to identify callers and the numbers they are calling from. (If you get the number, *do not call the person back and confront them about the call. This is ineffective.*) Your local telephone company's annoyance center can provide more information and assistance in stopping further obscene and harassing phone calls. Have your police report number available to provide the annoyance center.

Guide 5: Let the answering machine record obscene or harassing phone calls. The caller may be adamant about communicating with you and will want to leave a message on the answering machine. The taped message is evidence that needs to be given to the police.

Chapter 8
UNLAWFUL ATTACKS & SEXUAL ASSAULT

Ask yourself: Do I know how to avoid getting seriously injured by a violent assailant?

Local media, including campus newspapers, regularly report cases of assault and battery, sexual assault, and crimes involving firearms. In the United States, crimes of violence occur every day, in communities and on college campuses. College students are in the age group most likely to be the target of violent assaults. You may become involved in this statistic as a bystander who witnesses such an event, as a victim, or as an assailant.

Knowing the legal definitions of crimes will help you understand the elements of the criminal act. Dependent on the elements of the crime, assault is categorized as "simple assault" or "aggravated assault." The FBI's Uniform Crime Report defines simple assault as "an unlawful physical attack by one person upon another where neither the offender displays a weapon nor the victim suffers obvious severe or aggravated bodily injury involving apparent broken bones, loss of teeth, possible internal injuries, severe lacerations or loss of consciousness." Aggravated assault involves greater personal injury and may involve the use of a weapon. The UCR defines aggravated assault as, "an unlawful attack by one person upon another where either the offender displays a weapon or the victim suffers obvious severe or aggravated bodily injury involving apparently broken bones, loss of teeth, possible internal injury, severe laceration or loss of consciousness." In 1997, 500 colleges reported 1546 aggravated assaults to the FBI's UCR program, and 1558 aggravated assaults in 1998.

Your local police department or the state attorney's office can provide you with legal definitions for assault, and related state statutes. Accessing your state attorney's website may also provide this information. Some states, such as Florida and Georgia, have separate definitions for assault and for battery. In Florida, assault involves the intended and unlawful threat by word or act to do violence to another. The person has to have an imminent, apparent ability to commit the violence, creating fear in the victim. Battery involves the actual and intentional touching or striking of another person against their will to intentionally cause bodily harm. The severity of the violence and injury determines the level of the crime, aggravated assault, aggravated battery, or felony battery. In some states, a battery where the victim sustains a disabling injury, or loss of body parts, is referred to as "mayhem."

College students are more prone to be involved in an assault that involves alcohol and/or drug consumption, disorderly conduct, disturbance and affrays. Alcohol and drugs are significant contributors to assaults. According to U. S. Department of Justice statistics, four out of ten reported violent offenses involved the abuse of alcohol. *Binge drinking significantly increases the likelihood that you will be assaulted or will commit an assault and end up in jail.*

College Students Involvement in Violence

Where do college students get involved in violence? You can probably answer this question yourself: bar parking lots, concerts, outside sports stadiums after the "big game," and other such events. Events that involve large numbers of people and alcohol can become a scene of violence. Below you will find some scenarios, ranging from simple to complex.

Visualize yourself walking down the street after a football game or in the bar district. Two men walk toward you, punch you in the stomach and then flee. Do not verbally or physically antagonize the assailants. Do not chase them. Instead get away, find a safe place, get medical attention and report the incident to the police. Tell the police what the two men looked like and whether a weapon was involved. If the assailants left in a car, describe the vehicle and, when possible, give the license tag number. The direction they approached from and the direction where they fled is information that can help the police officer.

Now take this scenario and change it. You look across the street and see two men approaching another man, punching him in the stomach and fleeing in a blue Explorer. You are now a witness to an assault or battery. Any pertinent information you can provide to the police officer is important. As a safety smart student, call 9-1-1 immediately, to summon the police, and in a situation where an injury is sustained, also request an ambulance. Remain with the victim until the police arrive, since they will need to question you, to get the information they need to find the assailants.

Changing the scenario again, you and two of your male friends have a few beers while watching a college football game. After the game, the three of you decide to go out to a popular college bar and have a few more beers. As you and your friends are leaving the bar about 1:00 AM, two unknown males start yelling at you and calling you names. Instead of ignoring the comments and walking away, to avoid a confrontation, you and your friends decide to walk toward the males and start calling them offensive names also. The verbal comments turn physical when all five of you start punching and kicking each other. Unpredictably, one man decides to pull out a knife and stabs one of your friends. What situation do we have now? One man has committed aggravated assault and the rest of you have committed simple assault. We also have one man who has been injured in this fight. No one had planned to get involved in a fight, let alone be charged with a crime or become injured. The next morning, it may be your name printed in the paper, which is personally embarrassing.

How do you decide between "Fight and Flight"?

Being assaulted is dangerous and frightening. There is little time or opportunity to try to make the right decision, to either fight your assailant or to flee. Whenever possible, it is better to flee. Staying can heighten your risk of being seriously injured or killed. Multiple assailants complicate matters even more, and flight is certainly the safest avenue. Deciding whether to fight, to flee, to try to verbally de-escalate the assailant's violence, or to submit, is influenced by circumstances and by how an individual reacts to violence. How people react to threats or physical assault varies from individual to individual. Some people become immobilized by fear. Others get an "adrenaline rush" and fight back. Physical differences between the victim and the assailant are a factor. A 120-pound female, unskilled in self-defense tactics, throwing a punch at a 250-pound male weight lifter will not be advantageous. Other options include trying to talk calmly to the assailant, or running from the person and the danger.

Justifiable Use of Force

We have the right to use the amount of force needed to keep us from serious bodily harm or death. When using deadly force, be able to articulate the reasons why deadly force was needed for self-protection. In one scenario, a woman has a pocketknife and she uses the knife to stop a man from causing serious bodily injury to her. She has the right to protect herself from imminent, deadly force, but it is also crucial that she be able to provide the legal system, that is, the police and the courts, with a reasonable explanation of why that amount of force was necessary. The bottom line is to protect yourself the best you can and be prepared to justify any deadly force you use. It is better to have to justify your actions later than end up dead or seriously wounded.

Deciding to react with force or without force is an individual decision you make depending on the situation and circumstances, and on how you react and cope with violence. Unless you have already experienced it, you do not know how you will react and cope to violence until you are confronted with a real situation. Self-defense training for women, such as R.A.D., is offered by most colleges, enhances your physical abilities. Your instincts, safety skills, physical abilities and mental abilities are factors that influence how you will react to being attacked. Women, take the R.A.D. course to better prepare you for any potential dangerous person.

Alcohol's Bad Influence

Alcohol is a major contributor to violence. According to Bureau of Justice Statistics, three million violent crimes happen each year where victims perceived the offenders to have been drinking when the offense occurred. About 35% of violent crimes involve alcohol use by the offenders. The Department of Education reports that the number of on-campus liquor law violations involving criminal offense arrests for 1999 totaled 37,732. Disciplinary actions and judicial referrals involving liquor law violations totaled 128,682 for 1999.

Be Careful What You Say

When someone threatens you with violence, do not make inflammatory remarks or threats you cannot carry out. This will only put you, and everybody with you, into greater harm. During a confrontation with a violent person, or one who is impaired by alcohol or drugs, avoid escalating the person's volatile behavior. Your ego and pride can place you in more danger than you already are. You have nothing to prove at this point, but you can prove that you are smart by getting away from imminent danger. If you speak to the assailant, speak calmly, without provocation, with the intent to de-escalate the situation. Provocation will escalate the situation and the violence.

Everyone handles fear and reacts to fear differently. How a person self-manages fear influences the outcome of a violent situation. Try not to panic and make the best individual decisions you can under the circumstances. Do what is necessary to avoid being forced into greater danger. The two true stories below illustrate how a person in great fear dealt effectively with a horrifying, violent situation.

Survival Stories of Fear Transformed to Inner Strength

A young woman met a neighborhood acquaintance. She did not know him well, but they would periodically run into each other in the neighborhood park and they would engage in conversation. On one particular occasion, he asked her to go with him to the park. Feeling comfortable with her new neighborhood friend, she agreed. She does not know that he's a member of a gang. This seemingly harmless beginning had a horrifying outcome. A few gang members forcefully carried her into an abandoned building and repeatedly beat and sexually assaulted her. Knowing that her life was at stake, she made the personal decision to "play dead," by lying motionless on the dirt floor. As she lay in agony and pain on the dirt floor, the gang left her for dead. She knew they would eventually return. Although she could hardly move from the beatings, bleeding and pain, her desire to survive gave her the inner strength to crawl from the abandoned building to find safety and help. She is a survivor of horrible multiple violent crimes.

Another Survival Story

A young woman met a young man and soon after they went out on a date. On the first date, he wanted to meet her somewhere, other than picking her up at home and meeting her family. She accepted the terms and the first date was enjoyable. She was not hesitant about accepting another date with him, nor did she have any concerns about her safety. Once again, he wanted to meet her away from her home. On the second date, he brutally beat her in the back seat of his car, tied her up, put her in the trunk of his car and proceeded to drive to a desolate area with the intention to sexually assault and kill her. Knowing she would be raped and probably killed, she knew she had to somehow draw the attention of someone on the outside. As she lay tied and bound in the dark, closed trunk, the young woman managed to disconnect the vehicle's rear light wires in the trunk. Luckily, a police officer saw the vehicle and pulled her assailant over. The young woman heard the officer when he walked up to the car and she started making noises to let the officer know that she was in the trunk. This woman is a survivor of violence.

Recognize Potential Danger

Dating and associating with people you do not know well, drinking alcohol or using drugs all contribute to criminal opportunity and violence. Your ability to think clearly and make good decisions diminishes under the influence of alcohol and/or drugs. Eleven safety guides on how to avoid being assaulted or becoming an assailant are listed.

11 Safety Smart Guides to Avoid an Assault

Guide 1: Avoid dark, isolated places, especially when you are alone and also with friends.

Guide 2: Avoid fighting. Participating in a fight puts you in a precarious situation where you are no longer a witness, but are now one of the assailants.

Guide 3: Ego and pride can harm you more than help you in assault situations. Although you may want to prove a point, avoid participating in violence.

Guide 4: Always avoid indulging in alcohol or using drugs.

Guide 5: Avoid confrontation that will escalate an already bad situation.

Guide 6: Remove yourself when the potential for an assault is imminent.

Guide 7: Use your instincts, intelligence and physical ability to reduce your chances of becoming a victim of simple or aggravated assault.

Guide 8: Report incidents to police officials and provide them with as much information as possible. This helps police officers to apprehend your assailant.

Guide 9: When you are with a group of friends, avoid reacting to a challenging situation that will most likely turn into a fight.

Guide 10: Tune out any provoking and insulting comments made to you and your friends by others. Move on and remove yourself from a potentially bad situation.

Guide 11: Your life is more important than any property. When an assailant wants your money or other property, hand it over without confrontation or resistance.

RAPE: SEXUAL VIOLENCE

According to the U. S. Justice Department, 1.7 percent of college women are raped. The Sexual Victimization of College Women Report states that 48.8 percent of women whose experience fits the legal components of rape did not consider themselves victims of rape. This study also found that 4.7 percent of women who had been sexually assaulted did not know if they had been raped. A study conducted by the U.S. Department of Justice shows that, for every 10,000 college women, 350 are victims of attempted rape or rape. In January 2001, The Department of Education reported to Congress the following statistics for the years 1997, 1998, and 1999.

Sex Offenses (On-Campus)								
Forcible			Non-forcible			Total		
Public								
1997	1998	1999	1997	1998	1999	1997	1998	1999
1081	1138	1126	336	386	423	1417	1524	1549
Private (Non-profit)								
1997	1998	1999	1997	1998	1999	1997	1998	1999
584	629	698	123	169	189	707	798	887
Private (For-profit)								
1997	1998	1999	1997	1998	1999	1997	1998	1999
3	5	18	13	10	15	16	15	33

(U.S. Department of Education, Office of Postsecondary Education, A Report to Congress, 2001)

SSS Web reference: For a complete breakdown of this data, the web site is http://www.ope.ed.gov/security.

When you read or hear about a rape that has occurred on a college campus or community, it immediately instills fear about attending college and living in the community where the rape occurred. *Information is an antidote to fear.* Consider the following questions: What type of rape victimizes college students more, stranger or non-stranger rapes? When I ask you to visualize what a rapist looks like, how would you describe the rapist? When I ask you where a rape is most likely to occur, what picture do you draw in your mind? Is the rapist more often someone you know or a stranger? Most of us may be inclined to visualize a stranger, maybe a large man in dark clothes and wearing a mask to conceal his identity. We may visualize the rapist holding a knife or gun. He'll be lurking in the woods along jogging paths, or behind buildings at night, waiting for a woman walking alone. Does the visual scenario we have mentally drawn happen? Yes. Is this the most prevalent type of rape incident a college student may encounter? No. You are at greater risk of being raped by an acquaintance or someone you know. Non-stranger rape encompasses about 66 percent of all sexual assaults.

Incidents of sexual assault on college campuses are an increasing concern for students, parents, college administrators, the legal system and society as a whole. According to the National Institute of Justice and Bureau of Justice Statistics (NIJ)(BJS), about 3 percent of college women have been either raped or experienced attempted rape during a college year.

A federal law, know as the "Campus Sex Crimes Prevention Act", is important for college students to be familiar with. The Campus Sex Crimes Prevention Act amends Section 170101 of the Violent Crime Control and Law Enforcement Act of 1994. This law requires colleges and universities to give a statement to the campus community concerning registered sex offenders where law enforcement agency information provided by a State concerning registered sex offenders may be obtained. This notification requirement pertains to sexually violent offenders enrolled or employed by institutions of higher education in that state where the offender resides. This also includes giving notice of each change of enrollment or employment status of such person at an institution of higher education in that state. For more detailed information about this law, Security On Campus, Inc. provides this on their web site.

What is Rape? Who are the Victims? Who are the Rapists?

Rape is a violent crime against a person. With the rapist, it is about power and control, not sex. Women are predominantly the victims of rape, however no one is excluded from being targeted and victimized. Victims include females, males, various age groups, diverse nationalities, races, and socioeconomic and cultural groups. The rapist can be someone you know and trust, or someone you have never met. Being intuitive and cognizant about the potential opportunities for someone to commit rape is necessary in today's college environment.

The following information will provide you with sex offense definitions from the FBI's Uniform Crime Report.

Sex Offense Definitions

The FBI's UCR defines sex offenses that provide consistency within the legal system.

"Sex Offenses- Forcible" means "any sexual act directed against another person, forcibly and/or against that person's will; or not forcibly or against the person's will where the victim is incapable of giving consent."

"Forcible Rape" means "the carnal knowledge of a person, forcibly and/or against that person's will; or not forcibly or against the person's will where the victim is incapable of giving consent because of his/her temporary or permanent mental or physical incapacity or because of his/her youth."

"Forcible Sodomy" means "oral or anal sexual intercourse with another person, forcibly and/or against that person's will; or not forcibly against the person's will where the victim is incapable of giving consent because of his/her youth or because of his/her temporary or permanent mental or physical incapacity."

"Sexual Assault With An Object" means "the use of an object or instrument to unlawfully penetrate, however slightly, the genital or

95

anal openings of the body of another person, forcibly and/or against that person's will; or not forcibly or against the person's will where the victim is incapable of giving consent because of his/her youth or because of his/her temporary or permanent mental or physical incapacity."

"Forcible Fondling" means "the touching of the private body parts of another person for the purpose of sexual gratification, forcibly and/or against that person's will; or not forcibly or against the person's will where the victim is incapable of giving consent because of his/her youth or because of his/her temporary or permanent mental incapacity."

"Sex Offenses-Non-forcible" means "unlawful, non-forcible sexual intercourse." The two categories under non-forcible sex offenses are "incest" and "statutory rape". "Incest" means "non-forcible sexual intercourse between persons who are related to each other within the degrees wherein marriage is prohibited by law." "Statutory Rape" means, "non-forcible sexual intercourse with a person who is under the statutory age of consent." (Source: FBI Uniform Crime Reporting System.)

Rape is a serious violent crime against a person, causing emotional and physical trauma to the victim. A sense of personal violation, the after effects of trauma and a lack of trust in the judicial system are some reasons why victims are reluctant to report being raped. It is estimated that about 90 percent of rapes are not reported. The judicial system, police, victim service providers and hospital personnel are professionally trained to help you. Victim advocates are available to help you through the legal system, the medical exam process, and refer you to counseling and crisis intervention resources to help you cope with the aftermath and trauma. Victim advocates are also instrumental in helping you receive victim compensation for incurred expenses. Chapter 16 provides statewide and national contact phone numbers for these services. Reporting the crime and allowing professionals to help you through this traumatic personal experience is critical for your safety and overall health, both physically and mentally.

College living intensifies susceptible and vulnerable situations for criminal opportunity, including rape by someone known to you. According to a BJS/NIJ study, sexual assaults of college students occur more frequently after 6:00 PM. About 60 percent of such assaults occur on-campus in the victim's residence. Another 31 percent occur in other living facilities on-campus and 10 percent at fraternity houses. Most off-campus rapes occur in residences. A related concern is voluntary or involuntary illicit drug use. In situations involving alcohol or illicit drugs, women usually do not remember what happened or whether consent was given or not given. A stranger rape is more likely to be reported; non-stranger rape is frequently not reported.

The following information about rape focuses on non-stranger rape, the role played by alcohol and drugs in sexual assault, and what to do when you have been raped. Men cannot be excluded from this discussion. Social norms and expectations common to men influence how men perceive sex and women. Understanding men's learned behavior and what men need to know about the meaning of consent are discussed. Men must recognize the difference between consensual and nonconsensual sex, the risk of being accused of rape, and how it is possible to rape a woman and not realize that you are committing rape.

NON-STRANGER RAPE

College campuses and communities do experience more incidents of non-stranger rape compared to other types of rapes. This occurs at private and public colleges, large and small colleges, and colleges in both rural and urban areas throughout the United States.

Women are the primary victims of non-stranger rape, by men they know or have briefly met. The man that rapes or attempts to rape a woman may be the person you would least suspect of committing rape. A rapist may be the man next door, the man sitting near you in class, or a man you go out with once in awhile. According to BJS/NIJ, 90 percent of rape victims knew the offender. Most offenders are an acquaintance, friend, classmate or ex-boyfriend.

No one has the right to rape another person. Men who are accused of rape do not necessarily perceive themselves as rapists. Men, what you need to know is that engaging in sex with a woman without her consent is rape.

Drugs and alcohol add to the complexity of rape incidents. The rapist might resort to slipping a drug such as Rohypnol, GHB or

Ketamine into an intended victim's drink without her knowledge. These extremely dangerous drugs have a tranquilizing affect that sedates the person to the point of unconsciousness. These drugs can be found anywhere from the streets to the rave clubs where they are often used. High school and college age students have been using these drugs since the early 90s. More information about these drugs can be found in Chapter 12.

Become familiar with the following guides for dealing with rape, to be better prepared for any eventuality and so that you will know how to help someone else who has been raped.

Being a Rape Victim

Your safety is the most important consideration. Go to a safe place and tell someone that you have been raped. The police will help you, not blame or judge you. The police department is the first number to call for help. Other people to go to for help include friends, relatives, a rape crisis counselor, victim advocate, a counselor, a member of the clergy, an instructor, or anyone you feel most comfortable telling. *Do not deny that you have been raped, and do not take a shower or bath.* Taking a shower destroys evidence the police need for an arrest and conviction. Initially, a victim may not want to pursue criminal charges but may decide to later, after experiencing the initial trauma and fear. Do not delay, the sooner the better.

Immediate medical attention is needed, to treat any injuries that have been sustained. Many women are reluctant to take a sexual assault examination, but this is critically important. Nurses called Sexual Assault Nurse Examiners (SANE) are trained to do sexual assault examinations. Another important reason to report rape to the police is that, in most cases, a police investigator, and many times it will be a female police investigator, will go to the hospital to make sure the rape victim is okay and that everything is being done to help preserve evidence. Many college campuses have victim advocates that will also go to the hospital to help victims access the help and resources they need. Victim advocates are trained and experienced in sexual assault incidents and their intervention will help you through the process.

Evidence is critical in rape cases. The best time to collect physical evidence is within 72 hours of the incident. Also, the sooner you report being raped, the greater the chance of finding out whether a date rape drug was involved. Time is critical in detecting drugs in the body. A rape victim has to refrain from showering, washing, douching or changing clothes. In a situation where clothes have been changed, do not wash the clothes that were worn during the rape. Put the clothes – including shoes, socks and undergarments - in paper bags and give them to the police. Do not launder or remove any bed sheets, pillows, comforters, blankets, or rugs from the site where the rape occurred. Do not wash anything, until all evidence has been collected by the police. A police investigator will be assigned to investigate the rape. It is essential that you be honest and truthful in what you tell the investigator. The majority of police investigators are specially trained in sexual assault investigations. The rape victim and any witnesses are questioned about what happened. The suspect, when known, is also questioned, unless he invokes and wants an attorney.

Police investigators and police officers are never to judge you or make you feel embarrassed, but are mandated to focus on the investigation, to ascertain what happened and to establish "probable cause" to make an arrest. Evidence and testimony from you and witnesses are critical in establishing probable cause. "Probable cause" means that police officers have enough knowledge of facts and circumstances to warrant the belief that a suspect committed an offense.

Parental Notification

Most college students are 18 or older, so the law does not mandate parental consent or notification. When you reach 18 years of age, it is your decision whether to tell your parents or other family members about being raped. For some rape victims, telling their parents may be the best decision because it provides a close and trusted support system. Other victims may decide not to tell their parents. It is your choice and your wishes are to be honored. When you decide to inform your parents, remain in control of your situation and decision-making. You are the victim and what you need and want takes precedence.

99

This is difficult for many parents to understand because parents are protective of their children. Many of you resist telling your parents for a variety of reasons, such as fear of how they will react. You may be afraid they will blame you or you do not want to upset them. Some of you do not want to disclose to your parents that you are drinking alcohol, using drugs and/or going out to parties. Parents are the last ones you want to notify about these types of college activities. For those who feel they can tell their parents, it is a good decision to make. Initially, parents become upset or angry with what happened, but most parents can put that aside to be helpful and supportive, and this is what you need.

It is important that you depend on others to help you. As you go through the trauma stages, rely on the victim advocate and crisis intervention professionals to help you deal with the emotional and physical trauma. No one can do this alone, so get the support system that you need.

The thirteen safety guides will help reduce the chance of being a victim to a stranger or non-stranger rape.

13 Rape Prevention Guides

Guide 1: Avoid isolated places where a stranger can easily approach you. We have all heard tragic incidents where a young woman is jogging on a path in the early morning hours when no one else is around. The woman is later found in a wooded area, raped and killed.

Guide 2: Walk and jog with friends.

Guide 3: Never be too friendly with a stranger.

Guide 4: Never get into a stranger's vehicle, nor be alone with a person you do not know well.

Guide 5: Be careful not to share too much personal information with someone you do not know.

Guide 6: Always secure your home with strong locking devices.

Guide 7: Be aware of who and what is around you.

Guide 8: Friends look out for each other's safety when going out for the evening. The motto is: go out together, and come home together.

Guide 9: Stay away from excessive use of alcohol and drugs. Nighttime activities for many college students involve alcohol and/or illicit drugs. Your indulgence opens the opportunity for you to become a victim of rape. Since many college students are frequently going to parties and clubs where alcohol and drugs are present, know how to be safe from the criminal acts of others in such settings. Drinking too much or having someone put a drug in your drink without your knowledge makes you vulnerable and unaware of what is around you, who is around you, where you are and what you do. All these vulnerable behaviors are avoidable. Excessive drinking causes people to forget the night's events, and what decisions they have made. Some college women have expressed that alcohol was the prime contributor to their vulnerability and their decision to leave with a man they did not know well or know at all. After having a few shots of liquor with beer, for example, once intoxicated, not only does poor judgment happen, but you also will not remember what happened that evening or during the early morning hours. Be forthright with the investigator or detective that is helping you when asked about any alcohol consumption or drug use. The focus is the rape, not the alcohol or drugs, but also realize that the investigator will be inquiring about if you voluntarily or involuntarily consumed alcohol or used any drug. The investigator will need to know if someone forced you or did you voluntarily drink alcohol. Or did someone forcibly give you drugs without your consent or did you use drugs voluntarily? Did someone clandestinely, without your knowledge, drop a drug in your drink? Again, it is important to disclose this information to the investigator, and remember the focus is about the rape, not alcohol or drug usage.

Guide 10: Men are also vulnerable when they drink too much or use drugs. This is when bad decisions are made, such as the decision to force a woman to have sex. When you make such a decision, you are responsible and the consequences of rape will cost you dearly. Be smart and avoid these situations.

Guide 11: Communicate your sexual limits. It is normal to flirt and have fun. Men and women enjoy the attention and interest. When two people get together, both the man and woman have to establish a clear communication about sex. Women: when you do not want to have sex with a man, clearly communicate that to him and firmly tell him "no," that you are not consenting to sex. Say it! To just lay down and say nothing does not communicate to him that you do not want to engage in sex with him. Say it! "No." Sex cannot be a guessing game. Clear communication has to occur between both the woman and the man. Men, it is your responsibility to understand the meaning of "NO" and the meaning of "CONSENT". A woman who says "no" is not saying "maybe" or "I'm not sure." Take a "maybe" or a "not sure" as a "NO". A clearly verbalized "YES," where no drugs or alcohol are taken or given to her, she is an adult, meaning 18 years old or older and she is capable of giving consent knowingly, without mental and/or physical impairment are consensual factors. Nonverbal indicators are important to understand and recognize. For example, she's not saying no, but she's pushing you away. Her nonverbal reaction in pushing you away is telling you, "NO". The mere fact that she is intoxicated needs to tell you that she is impaired and not capable of consenting or not consenting to have sex with you. Your duty and obligation to this woman and to yourself is to stop and not to have sex with her. Peer intervention - helping each other not to make these kinds of bad decisions or take potentially dangerous risks – helps both men and women. Friends helping friends result in a happier and safer college experience.

Guide 12: Protect your drink. When you want a soda, ask for a can of soda that is not opened. Being handed a drink by someone else, especially when you do not know the person, is too risky – a drug may have been put in your drink. It happens more often than you may realize. Rave clubs and other similar types of dance clubs are arenas where predators are prone to slip drugs into someone's drink without her knowledge. Voluntary drug use is also prevalent at these clubs. Do not exclude the possibility that a bartender may decide to slip a drug into someone's drink. People assume that it is safe to accept a drink from a bartender. Unfortunately, it is not always safe, so watch the bartender as he prepares your drink. When you put your drink down and leave it unattended, that may be the opportunity someone is looking for. Disregard the drink and get another one. Men: think about the flip side of this situation. Who do you think will be the number one suspect when some man slips GHB into a woman's drink, and later in the evening you, without knowing she's been clandestinely dosed with GHB, end up taking her home and having sex with her? The number one suspect is not the unknown man who slipped the GHB into her drink; it is you!

Guide 13: Do not go home with someone you hardly know. To illustrate this point, let us present a situation where you and some friends are at a party and you have been drinking quite a bit and are intoxicated. Throughout most of the night, you and a woman have been flirting with each other. Before the evening ends you talk together and mutually decide to go back to your apartment. You know that she is intoxicated. The best decision is not to leave with her, nor take her back to your apartment. When going out in a group, help each other and make sure no one leaves with someone who is only an acquaintance, especially when alcohol has been consumed or drugs are used. Consistently practice going home safely together. Help one another stay safe. An excellent video about rape on campus for men and women is called, "Breaking the Silence." This video is available by Security On Campus. Contact information for Security On Campus can be found in Chapter 16.

Safety Smart Message for Women

Communicate your intentions and limitations about sex to the man you are with. Women, when a man wants to take you home late at night, or in the early morning after a night of partying, or when he calls you at 2:00 AM to visit him, it is not to talk. It is about sex! *Say "no" when you do not want to have sex.* Nonverbal gestures do not send a clear message to men. Express your intentions beforehand and when you do not want to have sex with a man, say, "no". Stay away from alcohol and drugs. It opens opportunities that you do not want and will later regret. Not remembering what happened and later wondering if you had consensual sex or not, will haunt you. No one has the right to pressure you or force you into having sex. Get away from anyone who tries to do this. Leave! You may have to fight to get away. The best practice is to not leave with any man, especially when you do not know him, after a party where most people have been drinking and wanting to hook up with someone to have sex. It is naïve to think that a man is taking you home after a party to talk and hold hands. It is about sex! Do not go to his place and do not let him go to your place, or anywhere else, when you do not want to have sex. It is dangerous to leave with someone you hardly know. We have all heard about the horrible endings these types of situations may have. Why take the risk? Be smart and stay away from drugs, alcohol and dangerous situations.

Safety Smart Message for Men

Most college men do not plan on going out to rape a woman. What makes men vulnerable to being accused of rape? Here are some causes: Poor communication between you and the woman, alcohol and/or drug use, peer pressure to "seduce and conquer," and how you are socialized to perceive gender issues. Men are socialized to be aggressive, win and conquer. Men are taught, as young boys, to be strong and aggressive. Unfortunately, some adult men teach young men that women are the lesser gender. This can be expressed through sports where the coach may say, "you throw the ball like a girl" or "you play sports like a girl". Statements such as these can adversely affect how young men view women and male/female relationships.

Being accused of rape, in and of itself, can tarnish your reputation and cause uncertainty about your character. Male athletic groups and fraternity groups have been known to harass or intimidate a woman when she reports that she has been raped by one of the team members or fraternity brothers. This constitutes further victimization and retaliation toward the victim and it is illegal. Before you decide to intimidate or threaten a woman because your buddy committed a crime and denies it, stop and think how you would feel if the rape victim was your sister, your girlfriend, or your mother. Would you want them intimidated, humiliated or threatened because they reported the rape?

Forcing or coercing a woman to have sex is not acceptable under any terms or conditions. You are responsible. You are a rapist when you force a woman to have sex with you or when you take advantage of the fact that drugs or alcohol impairs her and cannot intelligently and knowingly make the decision to consent or not consent. To avoid being accused of rape, establish a clear and open communication between you and the woman, so you know that you both are consenting to sex. Avoid trying a little harder to convince her to have sex with you. It is not a game and women never want to experience this personal violence.

Your personal responsibility involves not only taking good care of yourself, but also protecting a woman and yourself from a bad situation that later signifies rape. You may be aroused at the moment when you justify your actions, but there is no justification. The consequences are enormous and will impact you and the woman for the rest of your lives. An honorable man will never take advantage of a woman and will ensure she gets home safely where no one can take advantage of her. Be a gentleman, not a rapist.

Peer pressure and male group affiliations can weaken a person's fortitude to take a stand on what is right and wrong. Peer groups may promote what is right or may support what is wrong. Both individuals and their groups are responsible and accountable for their actions. Stand firm on right and justice instead of ignoring it or supporting injustice: be courageous.

The need to inform men about rape issues has prompted college programs designed to discuss these issues and problems. Take advantage of these programs and encourage your friends to do so also. One such program, The Men's Program, has been effective in educating men and giving men a new perspective about rape victimization.

The Men's Program

The Men's Program is for undergraduate college men. This program helps men to better understand and help women who have been raped. The program has proven to be effective with fraternity and athletic groups where it has changed men's attitudes toward rape. The college you attend may or may not have The Men's Program. The

University of Virginia in Charlottesville has one of the best and most recognized Men's Programs in the country, and can be a source of information about this program. Men who have participated in this program have found it to be a positive learning experience. The program helps men understand relationships with women better than before and leads to understanding how our culture and norms influence what we think and how we behave. Men who have participated in this program have commented that they now have better relationships with women because the communication is better. The program is not based on "male bashing" or "male blaming". It is a positive and informative experience for young men attending college.

Sexual Offender/Predator Registration

Sexual offenders/predators are dangerous and they are recidivists. They will continue to commit their crimes. In 1996, Congress passed the Magan's Law that gives citizens the right to know when a sexual offender/predator has moved into their community.

You need to know if a sexual offender/predator is living in your neighborhood and community, and this carries over to your needing to know if a sexual offender/predator is working at the college you are attending or is a student there. An important law that you need to know about is the Federal Campus Sex Crimes Prevention Act. This is a federal law that was enacted on October 28, 2002 requiring institutions of higher education to issue a statement to the campus community advising them about how they may obtain law enforcement agency information regarding sex offenders in the state. It also mandates sex offenders that are registered in a state, to provide notice to each institution of higher education that the person is employed, carries out a vocation, or is a student.

Many websites are listed on the Internet that will provide you with more information about sexual offenders/predators and registration. Your local sheriff's office or local police department are also two places you can inquire about if sexual offenders are in your community. Security On Campus, Inc. and also the KLAASKIDS Foundation are also two additional sources for more information. Listed are their website locations.

SSS **W**eb reference for Security on Campus, Inc.: http://www.securityoncampus.org/congress/cscpa.

SSS **W**eb reference for the KLAASKIDS Foundation: http://www.klaaskids.org/pg-legmeg.htm.

Chapter 9
THE DANGERS OF BEING STALKED

Ask Yourself:
Do I know how to protect myself against a stalker?

I s someone intentionally and repetitively following you or harassing
you? Is the person threatening you? Is this person putting you in
fear for your safety or the safety of others close to you? Are you
afraid that someone is going to physically harm you and has the
ability to do so? Being stalked is a frightening and potentially
dangerous situation. Stalking has been in existence for centuries,
however, prior to anti-stalking laws, such behaviors were dismissed as
annoying incidents. This ideology has changed.

What is Stalking?

Stalking is a crime whereby a person intrudes into another
person's life over a period of time in a way that permeates that
person's life with fear. The FBI's Uniform Crime Report defines
stalking as "an unlawful physical attack by one person upon another
after willfully, maliciously or repeatedly following the person. An
assault, where neither the offender displays a weapon, nor the victim
suffers obvious severe or aggravated bodily injury involving apparent
broken bones, loss of teeth, possible internal injuries, severe
laceration or loss of consciousness." Aggravated stalking is "an
unlawful attack, by one person upon another, after willfully and
maliciously or repeatedly stalking that person; an assault where either

the offender displays a weapon, or the victim suffers obvious severe or aggravated bodily injury involving apparently broken bones, loss of teeth, possible internal injury, severe laceration or loss of consciousness."

Anti-stalking laws did not come into effect in the United States until the 1990s. California spearheaded the first anti-stalking law, and other states followed. Such laws evolved when stalking became a more serious phenomenon in society, going beyond annoying behavior, and when love-obsessed stalkers targeted celebrities and other people of notoriety. Victimization is not limited to celebrities. Anyone, regardless of socioeconomic status, gender, notoriety or age can be a victim. Stalking laws vary from state to state. It is advantageous, as a college student, to be familiar with your state's stalking laws.

According to a National Violence Against Women Survey, 1 in every 12 women will be stalked and 1 in every 45 men will be stalked in their lifetime. Stalkers victimize about one million women and 370,000 men. One of the U. S. Department of Justice, Bureau of Justice Statistics (BJS) studies shows that the rate of victimization increases during the teen years, remains static at about 20 years of age, then begins to drop as a person gets older. The majority of college students are between the ages of 18 to 21, the age group most likely to become a victim of stalking.

SSS Web reference: A Stalking Assistance Site on the web provides statewide anti-stalking statutes. The web site is: http://www.stalkingassistance.com. This web site provides individual state statutes on stalking, definitions, elements of the crime and the level classification, either a misdemeanor or felony.

Stalking victims are prone to blame themselves for the stalker's behavior. It is important to realize that victims are not at fault; stalkers are at fault. Stalkers select their victims, not vice versa. Stalking behavior is not about love; it is about obsession and the need to have power and control over another person. Stalkers target anyone from total strangers to their intimate partners. Some types of stalkers are simple obsession stalkers, love obsession stalkers, intimate partner stalkers, erotomanic stalkers, serial stalkers, vengeful stalkers, false victimization syndrome stalkers, and the most recent, cyber-stalkers. Simple obsession stalkers perpetrate about 70 to 80 percent of stalking incidents and are also the type of stalker most likely to victimize college students. Simple obsession stalkers usually have had a personal and/or intimate relationship with their victims.

Stalkers take many different approaches in contacting their victims, such as threats, following, watching, phoning, emailing, gifts, messages, or other symbolic methods to get the desired attention from the victims. Victims of stalking do not solicit this behavior or want any of these contacts. The impact stalking has on a person and the people closely associated with the victim can adversely affect the individual's ability to live a normal, healthy life and reach their educational goals. Stalkers are unpredictable, complex and should not be lumped into one category. Stalkers have an obsession with their victim and feel they must have that person in their life.

Victims and Stalkers

Anyone can be a victim of stalking and anyone can be a stalker. Both women and men should be familiar with their state's anti-stalking laws, stalking behaviors and how to deal with stalkers. College life is a time when maybe you first experience your first love and first intimate relationship. Or you may have ended a relationship that you had in high school. College life involves new influences on personal development, to include many changes and meeting new people. Emotions and personal feelings are explored during this time in your life and may not always be fully understood. A new love is exciting. You feel light-hearted and happy. Another feeling you may not recognize is vulnerability. Emotions and thoughts focus on the new relationship and life as a couple. Time and energy are invested in the relationship. What can happen when one partner decides to end the relationship and the other person is having difficulty letting go? Instead of accepting the break up in a healthy and normal way, a potential stalker becomes obsessed and personally driven to get their ex-partner back into the relationship. Being stalked by an ex-partner can become a dangerous or lethal situation for the victim and others close to the victim.

Men are more often the stalkers and women are primarily the victims, but this does not exclude women from being stalkers. Both men and women can become unpredictably violent or vengeful when a relationship ends. Understanding stalking behaviors and different types of stalkers can help you deal with a stalking situation.

More About Stalkers

Obsession and possessiveness are the hallmarks of a stalker. A stalker wants to preserve a relationship or a non-existent fantasy relationship with an ex-partner, acquaintance or fantasy lover. The more desperate and hopeless the stalker feels about getting attention in their pursuit, the more dangerous he or she can become. It may begin with harassment or intimidation and may unpredictably escalate to violence. Incidents of domestic violence can also involve stalking by the partner who does not want to let go of the relationship. The stalker's motive is to coerce and influence the ex-partner back into the relationship. When this is not accomplished, a stalker may move on to another person or their rejection can lead to revenge and/or violence. You need to be aware that the stalker will tend to become more dangerous as the relationship dissipates and the ex-partner becomes more distant. *This is all the more reason to pay attention to who and what is around you and to report stalking incidents to the police.* Be familiar with campus, city and county law enforcement agencies and their phone numbers and locations. As mentioned above, stalker types include simple obsession stalkers, love obsessive stalkers, erotomania stalkers, false victimization syndrome stalkers and cyber-stalkers.

Simple obsession stalkers are usually associated with broken personal or intimate relationships. Simple obsession stalkers can turn out to be a roommate, classmate, coworker, friend, or acquaintance. An intimate relationship does not necessarily have to be a factor but this type of stalking commonly does evolve from intimate relationships. Simple obsession stalkers can become dangerous and vengeful when the relationship ends because they have put more time, energy and resources into the relationship, along with their self-identify and dependence on their partner. Simple obsession stalkers are the type most commonly encountered by college students, usually when one partner breaks off a relationship and the ex-boyfriend or ex-girlfriend is having difficulty letting go. Victims of stalking may find it difficult to understand their ex-partner's behaviors. It is not uncommon to feel sorry for your ex-partner and try to help him or her through their heartbreak and personal trauma. Before making this mistake, of trying to be their savior or healer, realize that stalkers are not motivated by their broken hearts or by loneliness. Stalkers are driven by the desire to maintain power and control over their ex-partners. Remember: it is about abnormal obsession and possession, not love. *Once the relationship is ended, firmly and explicitly communicate to your ex-partner that the relationship is over and you do not want him or her to make any contact with you. This message is to be communicated only one time.* When dealing with a stalker, avoid any negotiations or temporary reconciliation. This only adds fuel to a fire that can easily get out of control. Stalkers plan their manipulations and maneuvers to get their ex-partners to conform to their wishes to get back together. *When ending a relationship, sever the tie completely and move on with your life.*

Love obsession stalkers have no actual relationship with the person being stalked. Their target is usually a celebrity or other high profile person. Love obsession stalkers are different from simple obsession stalkers because no real relationship has ever existed with their victims. Love obsession stalkers have serious mental disorders and can become violent toward their victim. These stalkers may write letters, email, make harassing phone calls, or show up at places where they know the person will be. Love obsession stalkers can become dangerously frustrated when their fantasy does not play out as desired.

Erotomania stalkers believe their victim is in love with them. Women, not men, take the forefront in being erotomanic or delusional stalkers. In these situations, the erotomania stalker may have been briefly introduced to a person and then believes this new acquaintance has fallen in love with her or him. It is not unusual for erotomania stalkers to communicate with their perceived lover far more than is appropriate for the level of acquaintance. For example, a college woman believes that her history professor is in love with her and she becomes overly personal when she talks to him. She may try to reach him by phone, email or show up at college-related events where she knows he will be. Erotomanic stalkers are not as likely to harm their victim as other types of stalkers, but the potential of harm should not be ruled out.

False victimization syndrome stalkers create fictitious incidents, portraying themselves to be victims of stalking or other crimes. The false victimization syndrome stalker's objective in fabricating such stories is to get the attention of their partner who is about to end the relationship or has already done so. False victimization syndrome is not as prevalent as the other types of stalking, making up about two percent of stalking cases. False victim stalkers are more often women, not men. False victim stalkers often make false police reports of stalking or assaults, giving detailed descriptions of their self-created stalker or assailant. To illustrate this, a woman dates a man for a few months and later becomes obsessed with him during and after the relationship. She is attending college for the first time and he was her first significant boyfriend. After a few months of dating, he ends the relationship with her. Two days later she reports to the police that an unknown man attacked her. This was the first of several police reports she fabricated to get her ex-boyfriend back. Her ex-boyfriend becomes increasingly worried for her personal safety and begins to stay with her to protect her most of the day and night, which is exactly what she wants. This type of stalker not only impacts her ex-partner, but also roommates and family. Her roommates are in fear for their safety, causing adverse affects in their ability to conduct their daily activities. Anyone who contemplates using this tactic to get their ex-boyfriend or ex-girlfriend back needs to realize that it is a crime to make false police reports, and the restitution you will pay for police services can be astronomical.

Cyber-stalkers use the Internet to stalk their victims, using chat rooms, email or newsgroups. This is known as cyber-stalking. Cyber-stalkers are more often male perpetrators and victims are usually female, although women too can be cyber-stalkers. Cyber-stalkers, like all the other types of stalkers, are abnormal and potentially dangerous. Cyber-stalkers are driven to gain power and control over another person through electronic communication. This can involve harassing, threatening, or hateful communications that cause a person to be in fear. This situation has the potential to escalate when a predator obtains more personal information about the victim.

Pragmatically, the solution is to be as anonymous as possible, not relinquish personal information about you and avoid entering web sites that inadvertently or blatantly suggest promiscuous behaviors or sexual connotations. Chapter 15 discusses personal safety and the Internet.

Anyone who is being harassed, intimidated or threatened through electronic communications should report these incidents to the police in the jurisdiction where the communication is occurring. Retain both the hard copy of the communication being sent to you and the digital copy for tracing purposes. It is important to tell the police the exact threat that is being communicated by this person. Two issues - repetitiveness and the credibility of the threat communicated by the cyber-stalker - are factors defining cyber-stalking crimes, with some variations from state to state. Identifying Internet predators can be difficult, especially when the stalker is clever about maintaining anonymity. Cyber-stalkers can be anyone, from anywhere, known or not known to you. Computer crimes that cross state lines are under the jurisdiction of the Federal Bureau of Investigations (FBI) and federal law addresses interstate stalking. You do not have to live in fear. Empower yourself by taking control of the situation and work toward a solution by involving police professionals.

Does a person deal with cyber-stalkers the same way as other types of stalkers? Yes. Although a cyber-stalker may or may not be physically near you, the stalker may seek a closer encounter when he or she learns more about you. *Do not communicate with this person at all.* Further communication with a stalker encourages a continuation of the stalking. Cyber-stalkers are not only potentially dangerous, but are able to hide their true identify from you and others. Cyber-stalkers can be anyone from a person you know to a person you never met. They can be anywhere, across the country or living next door. A cyber-stalker's true identify is usually not disclosed, nor their intentions. You are blindfolded to who the person really is and what the person is capable of. Cyber-stalkers want to find out as much about you as they can. More information about cyber-stalking can be found in Chapter 15, including how a computer name can symbolize a person's character to others and increase their chances of becoming a target.

If you enjoy communicating with various newsgroups, chat groups and email correspondents, avoid sites that solicit behaviors a cyber-stalker will look for, such as sexual deviant behaviors. Keep your personal information to yourself when corresponding on the Internet. This includes your age, address, phone number, marital status, whether you have children, where you socialize, where you work, what church you attend, what college you attend or any other personal information that strangers do not need to know. The information you give out to others can be used against you in many ways. Cyber predators can use personal details about you to spread bogus information about you over the Internet, opening the door for more predators to seek you out. The possibilities for crime are too great to take such a risk. Select chat groups, newsgroups and/or email correspondents cautiously and refrain from sharing personal information. Hopefully, you will not encounter a cyber-stalker or any other type of stalker. If you do, deal consistently with stalkers and practice the safety guides given. Certain warning signs can surface during a relationship that signals a potential for stalking.

Stalker Characteristics

Potential stalkers may demonstrate certain personal characteristics during a relationship. Detecting these traits can provide some early warning that this person could turn out to be a stalker when the relationship ends. Stalkers come from various cultural backgrounds, occupations and socioeconomic levels. They can be male or female and of various ages. You are not able to identify a stalker by his or her appearance. What does help is being attentive to how this person behaves. Behaviors and personality traits of a potential stalker include, but are not limited to, the characteristics listed below. Detecting a cluster of these characteristics in a partner or ex-partner is a danger signal to be aware of.

- Insecurity
- Low self-esteem
- Jealousy
- Dominance
- Self-perception of being inadequate
- Emotional impairment
- Abusive behavior (emotional and/or physical, verbal or non-verbal)
- Lack of self-confidence
- Obsession

- Possessiveness
- Excessive behavior
- Infatuation with partner or ex-partner
- Unstable emotions
- Volatile propensity to violence
- Distrust of you and others
- Tendency to be a loner
- Codependent
- Manipulates through coercion
- Difficulty dealing with rejection
- Power and control driven

A person who has a cluster of the characteristics mentioned above is a person who may have difficulty accepting the end of a relationship. This person can become dangerous and volatile when a relationship ends. It is unwise to underestimate the dangers involved in any stalking situation. Since stalking is a terrorizing experience, a person's ability to explain to police officers what she or he is feeling (i.e., frightened) and what is happening (i.e., for two weeks, he has been following me to my work every morning) is paramount. Feeling threatened, terrorized, scared and fearful of your life is your inner alarm system warning you to be attentive and aware of this person. Report incidents of stalking to the police and the college's victim advocate. Try to explain what the stalker is doing that is causing you to feel this way. Who is stalking you, where you are being stalked, what days and times you are being stalked, how you are being stalked, and why this person is stalking you - all this is vital information to share with the police.

The goal is to stop the stalker and keep you safe from further threat and harm. The eighteen safety guides will help you deal with a stalking situation more effectively.

18 Safety Smart Guides About Stalking

Guide 1: Be attentive to the personality traits and behaviors of your partner. Signs of possessiveness, obsession, jealousy, dominance, power and control are early warning signs that this person could become a stalker.

Guide 2: Do not feel sorry for a stalker and attempt to appease his or her broken heart. The stalker's torment is not about love, it is about their loss of power and control. When dealing with an ex-partner who is displaying stalking behaviors, it is essential to firmly and explicitly communicate that the relationship is over and he or she is not to make contact with you in any way. This has to be a one-time message to the stalker. Any communication, even if it is negative, is better then none to the stalker, and it also encourages further stalking.

Guide 3: Do not be alone or in an isolated area with a potential stalker when you break off the relationship.

Guide 4: Know the anti-stalking law in your state. This is critical to your ability to effectively articulate what has happened, what is happening, and what the stalker is doing that constitutes stalking.

Guide 5: Immediately contact the police in all stalking situations. Stalking incidents across jurisdictional boundaries, such as in the city, county and campus areas, necessitates you contacting each individual law enforcement agency and reporting each incident separately. Inform each agency that you have reported stalking incidents in the other jurisdictions.

Guide 6: Colleges and/or communities offer victim services that can be effective in helping stalking victims through the legal system and giving them emotional support. Victim advocates, as well as police officers, are sources to help you obtain a restraining order from the court. Victim advocates are professionally trained to understand and support the emotional and physical trauma experienced by victims of crime. During your college assessment and selection process, find out where the victim services office is located, the name of the victim advocate and the phone number for this person. Victim advocates are usually available 24-hours a day, seven days a week. Use this resource when you feel threatened and in fear because of someone else's violent or threatening behaviors toward you.

Guide 7: Cellular phones provide an immediate means to contact police when a dangerous situation occurs. College campuses also have emergency phones located throughout the campus. Blue phones are easily identifiable because of the blue light and the word EMERGENCY printed in large letters on the base of the phone.

Guide 8: A stalker may decide to get near your home or break into your home. Ensure that you have home safety features, such as extra locking devices on windows, doors and sliding glass doors. Chapter 3 provides more information about residential safety and security.

Guide 9: When traveling - walking, driving, biking and so on - use alternate routes so that your travel is not predictable to the stalker. Do not choose routes through isolated areas. Be able to access your vehicle without delay and look around as you approach your vehicle. Observe the ground near your parked vehicle, other vehicles parked nearby and look inside your vehicle before entering – these are safety smart practices. Immediately go to a safe place when the stalker is waiting for you.

Guide 10: You do not have to be embarrassed or clandestine about being stalked. Tell friends, bosses, instructors, apartment managers, housing officials, coworkers, classmates, roommates and your family that you are being stalked. If possible, provide others with a picture or description of the stalker so they can recognize the person in the event he or she is nearby or enters a building looking for you. For stranger stalkers, any personal identification information or vehicle information is important to provide police and others.

Guide 11: Ask others not to give out any personal information about you. Stalkers are clever about getting personal information and will solicit information from roommates, friends, family and others.

Guide 12: Stalkers sometimes resort to using the telephone to make contact with their victims. Obtain an unlisted phone number with a separate phone line, and keep your original phone number hooked up to an answering machine to take the calls. Give the unlisted phone number to close friends and relatives that you trust not to give this information to others. The listed phone number with the answering machine is to record the stalker's calls as evidence for the police. Refrain from answering this phone; instead use an answering machine.

Guide 13: Keep an information log to document each time the stalker tries to initiate contact with you. Provide the detective or investigator assigned to your case a copy of the log, the answering machine tapes, caller-identification information and any other information that can help with the investigation.

Guide 14: Consider getting a restraining order. Always have the restraining order readily available to provide to police officials when needed. A restraining order is useful because it involves the legal system ordering the stalker to stay away from you. Realize that this does not guarantee your safety because the stalker may ignore the order or his or her anger may intensify when receiving the restraining order.

Guide 15: Colleges offer nighttime escort service to and from college buildings and parking lots. Use this service when you need extra protection in your travels on campus.

Guide 16: Some stalkers will send gifts or cards in the mail or leave them on your doorstep. Do not open these cards or gifts. Give them to the police. Such items become more evidence in the stalking case.

Guide 17: Be with friends or others as much as possible. Try not to be alone, to give the stalker the opportunity to get close to you.

Guide 18: Cyber-stalking incidents should be handled in a similar way to other stalking situations. Because you cannot see the stalker and do not know his or her identity, does not mean that you are safe.

A Final Message About Stalking

NEVER trust a stalker and take stalking seriously. Do not feel sorry for the stalker and try to appease him or her; this does not make things better and can make matters worse. Confide in close friends or family members that you trust for emotional support and help. Police officers and detectives are trained to assist you with stalking incidents. When you contact the police to report the crime, offer as much information as possible - who is stalking you, what the person is doing and/or saying to you that is threatening, when and where the stalking occurs and any other circumstances about the stalking. To recall information as accurately and concisely as possible, maintain a written record of when and where the stalking happens, and what the person is saying and doing to cause you discomfort and fear for your personal safety. For stalkers who are unknown to you, describe anything you find out about the person to the police. Do not approach or try to reason with the stalker. You are dealing with an abnormal person who might become unpredictably violent toward you and the people around you.

A message for potential stalkers: BEWARE. Stalking is a serious crime. If you are having difficulty accepting the end of a relationship, be careful not to become a stalker yourself. Review the characteristics and behaviors of the stalker and recognize that you may have some traits that can lead you down a path of stalking your ex-partner. Your objective must be to accept the end of a relationship and move on in a healthy manner, without committing unlawful acts. If necessary, seek professional help in overcoming and dealing with an ended relationship. Crossing the line into stalking will impede your educational goals, along with landing you in jail with a criminal record.

**Do not stalk your girlfriend or boyfriend when the relationship ends.
Stalking is a crime**

Chapter 10
A CLANDESTINE CRIME:DOMESTIC VIOLENCE

Ask Yourself: Am I afraid of my partner?

Our home should be our safest and most secure place, our haven. The people who share our lives and household should be the people who care the most about us and want us to be safe and happy. A loving and nurturing home environment is a right, not a privilege. Absolutely no one deserves to be a victim of abuse and violence. Domestic violence is a crime that severely damages the individual, the family and society as a whole. Domestic violence cannot be ignored nor can this crime remain clandestine. There are laws, programs and support systems available to end domestic violence by helping victims and arresting and prosecuting the abusers. Nevertheless, we have a lot of work ahead of us to end domestic violence. Victims, citizens, victim services, private and public organizations, the legal system and educators have to work together to end the violence. Victim compensation, shelters, proactive law enforcement, educational programs and domestic violence laws exemplify some of the components required to end domestic violence in our communities.

What is Domestic Violence?

Domestic violence involves physical, emotional, and/or sexual violence. Domestic violence is about power and control over another person. Abusers within the home use violence to create fear in their victims, manipulate their victims and control resources such as money and vehicles to maximize their power and control over their partners and to isolate their partners from others. Domestic violence is about destroying another person's self-esteem and self-confidence.

Domestic violence takes place within households and involves the crimes of assault, battery, sexual battery or any other criminal act that results in physical injury or death inflicted by a present or former member of the household. Domestic violence does not apply only to married people. Domestic violence occurs among divorced people, people who are dating, and people who are cohabiting or have cohabited in the past. This form of violence affects children and other family members. Each state has its own definition of domestic violence and state laws pertaining to domestic violence. Become familiar with your state's domestic violence laws.

Who are the Victims of Domestic Violence?

Domestic violence victimization is not exclusive but inclusive. Victims include women and men, people of various ages, and people from a wide range of socioeconomic, educational, religious and cultural backgrounds. College students are not exempt from domestic violence. According to the U. S. Department of Justice, between 1993 and 1998, women between the ages of 16 and 24 experienced the highest per capita rates of intimate violence. Another way to state this is that 19.6 women per every 1000 women in this age group became victims of domestic violence. College age women experience the highest rates of intimate violence. A Justice Department study reports that in 1998 about 876,340 women were victims of domestic violence compared to about 157,330 men. Of the intimate partner relationships that involve violence, women were victimized five times more often than men. Women are more apt to be victimized by someone they know, such as a friend, family member or intimate partner as opposed to men who are more apt to be victimized by a stranger. According to a U. S. National Crime Survey (NCS) about 84 percent of victims of intimate violence are women. Women are the primary victims of domestic violence and men are the primary perpetrators. According to the 1995 Bureau of Justice Statistics, National Crime Victimization Survey, women are victims of intimate-partner attacks six times more often than men.

Male Victims of Domestic Violence

Although women are the primary victims of domestic violence, men are also victimized. Men are more reluctant to report domestic violence, primarily because of societal stereotypes of men, who are supposed to be rough and tough. It is embarrassing for a man to report being beaten by a woman. In addition, men fail to report domestic violence for the same reasons women fail to report this crime. Abusers blame their partners and manipulate their partners into believing the violence is their fault. Abusers reject personal blame or accountability for their violent acts. Another emotional ploy is "you're a man, you can take it." Female abusers, like male abusers, seek power and control over their partners.

Abused men also feel fear, embarrassment, shame, damaged self-esteem and lack of confidence because of the emotional and physical abuse from their partners. The perception that they will be laughed at or not believed is a real experience for the male victim of domestic violence. Both men and women need to understand domestic violence and be protected from it. All victims of domestic violence are encouraged to report incidents of domestic violence to the police.

The Clandestine Crime

Victims of domestic violence are confronted with certain barriers that distract or discourage them from reporting incidents to their friends, family, crisis centers, or the police. FEAR is the primary reason women refrain from telling anyone about the violence. That is one significant reason why this crime is clandestine. Victims not only fear for themselves, but also for the safety of their children and other family members. Victims may fear that no one will believe them, fear being judged, or think that what is happening to them is not all that serious. Since abusers usually control the finances and control their partners both socially and psychologically, it is difficult and fearful for a victim to consider leaving the perpetrator.

In 1997, The Federal Office of the Status of Women (OSW) conducted a study about how women survive domestic violence. The OSW has identified multiple reasons why victims may not seek help: denial or disbelief about what is happening to them, love for their partner, belief that the violent behavior will stop, shame and embarrassment, concerns for children, depression, stress and isolation. Victims of domestic violence may feel that others are unable to help, or believe that domestic violence is a personal problem that needs to be dealt with independently, without crisis intervention, victim services or the police. When a person reaches the point where she can no longer cope with the abuse, or a crisis occurs when the abuser seriously injures his partner, the violence begins to unveil itself.

Abusers Want to Keep Their Violence Hidden

The abuser's primary motive for wanting to keep his crimes hidden is, once again, power and control. The abuser's violence is fueled by the need to maintain power and control over his partner. The abuser knows the violence is a crime and does not want anyone to find out about the violence for fear of being arrested, losing the partner and losing power and control over that partner's life. Why do you think abusers isolate their partners? Reasons include jealousy, possessiveness and a need to hide the violence. Since abusers justify their violence and blame their partners for the violence, this hidden form of violence will not end until the abuser takes responsibility for his or her violent behavior and seeks professional help.

Who are the Domestic Violence Abusers?

The crime of domestic violence is inclusive. Although men are reported to be the dominant perpetrators of domestic violence, women are offenders too. Abusers come from all different nationalities, socioeconomic groups, age groups, cultures, races, and religions. Today law enforcement takes a proactive role by arresting the primary offender. It is no longer assumed that the primary offender is always the man or that domestic violence happens only in working class households. Domestic violence can be happening to anyone, in any neighborhood.

Know the Risk in Staying and the Safe Way to Leave

There is a big risk involved in staying in a violent household, because the violence will only continue and has the potential of escalating to serious injury or death. The longer anyone stays in this situation, the more his or her self-esteem and self-confidence are damaged, making it that much harder to leave. Those with children need to be aware of the danger children are also being exposed to. Children who live in violent households are also victims. Unlike physical injuries, emotional damage is not visible, but emotional damage is as painful, if not more, than physical pain.

If you are a victim of domestic violence, formulate a step-by-step plan for leaving the violence and finding a safe, healthy and happy environment. The safety smart plan presented below is only a framework of steps that can assist you in leaving the abuser. These steps are not etched in stone but are factors to consider when planning on leaving an abusive and dangerous partner. The primary goal is to get away from the violence as soon and as safely as possible. How do you do this? Develop a safe plan to leave, based on the four powerful safety smart "P's": PLAN, PREPARE, PERSEVERE and PROTECT.

> * PLAN: Confide in a trusted friend or family member and get the help you need when you are planning to leave.
> * PREPARE: Save money, pack some clothes, and gather personal necessities without your partner knowing. Make any other necessary preparations, such as finding a method of transportation away from the abuser.
> * PERSEVERE: You will feel fear and self-doubt as you plan and prepare. The abuser may ask for forgiveness, promise to never hurt you again, or shower you with gifts. These tactics are a ploy to keep you in the grip of violence along with keeping you in your place as dictated by the abuser. Persevere means, "to persist in anything undertaken in spite of difficulty or obstacles."
> * PROTECT: Self-protection and protection of children, during the planning phase and afterwards, is essential to safeguard against continued violence from your partner.

Move Forward, Not Backward

Leaving an abusive relationship is difficult and frightening. Unknown obstacles are encountered when you detach yourself from a violent existence. It is helpful to understand the patterns involved in an abusive relationship, when deciding whether to leave. Violence-prone individuals have the propensity to show similar behaviors in their abuse towards their partner. Take a few minutes and ask yourself some provoking questions about how you are being treated by your partner. "Yes" responses should indicate to you that your emotional and physical wellness is at risk, and you are in an abusive relationship.

Are you interrogated about how you spend your time and where you go?
Are you accused of cheating on your partner?
Does your partner control the financial resources?
Does your partner insult you when alone or in front of others?
Does your partner hit you?
Does your partner become angry and damage property?
Are you removed from your friends and family?
Are you limited in your activities, such as, work or school?
Are you criticized about your appearance?
Does your partner tell you what you will wear?
Does your partner abuse alcohol and/or use drugs?
Are you forced to have sex?
Does your partner also abuse your children?
Do you feel depressed or fearful of your partner?
Do you feel lonely and isolated from others?
Do you lack self-esteem?

Abusive people will use manipulative tactics to acquire power and control over others. This is accomplished in several ways, to include, intimidation, coercion, threats, emotional abuse, physical, isolation, using your children, controlling economic resources, dictating male dominance, and minimizing the abuse by turning it around and blaming you.

Does this sound like a vicious circle? It does evolve into a repetitive cycle. Now, compare this to a healthy relationship. What are the components of a healthy relationship, without violence? A good relationship is a relationship where love, respect, trust, support, honesty, fairness, sharing responsibilities and mutual accountability are continual characteristics.

A plan of action is needed to get out of a bad relationship and to help you get away from the violence as safely as possible. Your ultimate goal is to stop the violence. The safety guides presented are steps to take when you want to leave an abusive situation and violent person. A perfect plan is never etched in stone, as every individual has their own needs and requirements. These eight guides are suggestions to help victims of domestic violence, and to be able to begin a new life that brings happiness, independence and safety.

8 Safety Smart Guides to Leave an Abusive Relationship

Guide 1: The abuser must never be aware of your plan to leave. The abuser's knowledge of this can become a catalyst for continued and unpredictable violence. Plan quietly and share your plan only with a trusted confidant who will not disclose the plan to the abuser or anyone else.

Guide 2: Recognize that you, your family members and your friends are susceptible to danger from the abuser's violent behavior. Try to secretly put away some money without it being noticed. Have personal belongings ready to go at all times. Prepare for departure when the abuser is not home, and when possible have a friend or family member there when you leave.

Guide 3: Planning to leave involves having a safe place to go. Staying in your home is not an option when violence is imminent. Prepare to have a safe place to go to. For those with children, your plan and preparation involves their safety and getting them away from the violence. Your local victim services center is an excellent resource. Victims advocates will help you with injunctions, refer you to a temporary shelter for you and your children and connect you with other resources needed to make the transition as safe as possible.

Chapter 16 lists resources that you can access to help you get away from an abusive partner.

Guide 4: Report domestic violence to the police. If you are fearful about calling the police on your own, confide in a good friend, family member, clergy person or victim advocate. Many victims do not want to have charges filed on their partner, nor do they want them to go to jail. Victims of domestic violence are not at fault; their abusive partners are at fault and need to be arrested. The fear and intimidation tactics used by an abusive partner can keep an abused person from wanting the abuser arrested. Although it may not be apparent to you at the time, police intervention in arresting an abusive partner can be the first step toward that person finally getting the help he or she needs. Remain steadfast and let the events take their needed course.

Guide 5: Depend on others to help you through this process. Feelings of fear, anxiety, self-doubt and trauma are strong as one makes this transition. Use the resources available to help you obtain the life that you need and deserve. As previously mentioned, police and victim advocates can help domestic violence victims get a restraining order against their abusers. A restraining order does not guarantee the violent partner will abide by the terms of the order. Restraining orders apply not only to the home, but can also be stipulated to include work, school and other places you frequent.

Guide 6: Be familiar with the domestic violence laws and judicial processes in your state.

Guide 7: More often than not, an abusive and violent partner will try to get back into a relationship with his or her partner. He or she will promise that the battering and violence will stop. The victim will be told how much they are loved. Love never involves battering and violence. Avoid temptation and refrain from weakening. Stand your ground and be strong in your personal convictions. The violence will not stop when you stay. After all, the violent person does not perceive himself or herself as the problem. Professional intervention is needed to stop these people from continual violent behavior. Many victims of domestic violence go back to the violence several times before acquiring the fortitude and strength to be steadfast in their decision to move on and make a happier and safer life for themselves.

Guide 8: Never trust your partner's tactics to get you back or be near you. Once you leave, avoid any communication or interaction. This person is not your friend and is not looking out for your best interests. He or she has proven this to you time and time again. Recognize that he or she can become more dangerous to you and possibly others around you, so be as safety conscious as possible.

End the Cycle of Violence

Throughout history, domestic violence has been a cancer within society, and it still is a serious, damaging, social ill that affects individuals, families, and society as a whole. A clandestine crime, the violence is hidden within the privacy of the home. When the violence is revealed, victims of domestic abuse begin to gain the strength and fortitude to leave the lifestyle of violence. Is this difficult to accomplish? For the many reasons we have identified, yes, it is. These hurdles are difficult to overcome but they can and must be conquered. The key is to find the strength, courage, and support system necessary to move on to a safer and happier life style where violence does not exist. You deserve a life that includes being treated with respect, care and kindness. NEVER settle for less.

Chapter 11
SEXUAL HARASSMENT

Ask yourself: Do I know how to stop being sexually harassed?

No one has the right to abuse his or her position to violate another person. Sexual harassment is in violation of Title VII of the Civil Rights Act of 1964, and Title IX of the Education Amendments Act of 1972. The Equal Employment Opportunity Commission (EEOC) promulgates, sexual harassment is a form of sex discrimination. Sexual harassment occurs in the highest levels of government down to the smallest organizations in America. Sexual harassment is wrong. There is no justification for this behavior and it should never be permitted in our workplaces and academic environments. Unfortunately, the problem of sexual harassment continues to plague our work and learning environments. College students and other victims of sexual harassment are often apprehensive about reporting sexual harassment to college officials, such as the director or dean of students. Reasons for this include fear of losing their jobs, fear of retaliation from management and peers, fear of social isolation for reporting harassment, self-blame, or fear of being perceived as a troublemaker. In an academic setting, as a student, you may fear failing the course, perceive that the instructor may be believed more than you will be, and feel embarrassed and fearful. In our society, young people are taught to respect their elders and to trust teachers and employers as people who guide students in their academic and career-related endeavors. College students who are victims of sexual harassment by an adult, especially an authority figure, magnify their fear and anxiety in trying to cope with the harassment. A student sexually harassed by another student also experiences fear and anxiety.

Sexual harassment is abuse of power over another person. Do you have recourse when sexually harassed in the workplace or academic environment? Yes. Employers and colleges have stringent policies and procedures against sexual harassment. Also, the EEOC conducts investigative inquiries into sexual harassment incidents. As a student, you have important goals. Sexual harassment has the potential to poison the very wellsprings of your sense of meaning and purpose. An understanding of what sexual harassment is and what steps can be taken to stop sexual harassment will support your courage and ability to take the step of reporting sexual harassment to college officials.

Sexual harassment is damaging and threatening to personal and educational experiences. No student, faculty or staff member should ever have to tolerate sexual harassment. Definitions of what constitutes sexual harassment are similar from one college to another, where policies and procedures for reporting and investigating sexual harassment differ slightly. Colleges have standards set against sexual harassment and processes in place to investigate allegations of sexual harassment. Become familiar with the policies and procedures at the college you attend, along with federal laws prohibiting sexual harassment. The college you attend should include this information in your student orientation information packet. If not, ask for this information.

What is Sexual Harassment?

Sexual harassment is unwelcome sexual advances, requests for sexual favors, or other behavior of a sexual nature. Compliance with such conduct is a term or condition of an individual's employment or academic participation, either explicitly or implicitly. Submission to or rejection of such conduct may be used as the basis for decisions affecting an individual's employment or academic career, or participation in college functions. Sexual harassment is conduct that creates an intimidating, hostile or offensive environment.

You and every other student should report incidents of sexual harassment. You need to be clearly and effectively informed that sexual harassment is not tolerated at your institution. You must also have a clear understanding of how to report allegations and what to expect through the process. Effective sexual harassment policy encourages students to report incidents of sexual harassment, not only personal encounters, but also incidents that involve another student who is being sexually harassed. Report sexual harassment incidents immediately to the dean of students or other designated college officials. The objective is to stop sexual harassment, find resolution and have appropriate corrective action taken. If you do not feel confident reporting the incident to a designated college official, go to someone you do trust, perhaps a professor or housing adviser, and report the sexual harassment.

It is the responsibility of the college to investigate all complaints of sexual harassment, through fair and impartial procedures that prove or disprove sexual harassment allegations. Sexual harassment investigations are confidential while the investigation is active. Public record laws do vary from state to state; inquire about public record laws pertaining to sexual harassment complaints and investigations. Be aware that information about the investigation is disclosed to the accused party and other witnesses in order to gather facts and evidence in the case. The accused person has the right to know the offense that he or she is being accused of and the complainant's name. Any retaliation or discrimination toward the complainant should immediately be reported to college officials.

When the investigation is completed and reviewed by appropriate college officials, the complainant is informed in writing of the findings of the investigation. If the complainant is not satisfied with the results of the college investigation, there are other avenues available, such as through grievance procedures, administrative hearings, or legal processes (i.e., EEOC, retaining an attorney). College procedures should include resolution processes that are available to the complainant, which may include an appeals process. First, give your college the opportunity to investigate and resolve incidents of sexual harassment. Colleges have an affirmative action officer who oversees all sexual harassment investigations. This person is another resource to help with sexual harassment incidents in a college environment. In short, U. S. colleges do not tolerate sexual harassment and victims of sexual harassment have recourse.

How do you know when you are being sexually harassed?

Sexual harassment can be subtle or overt. You can hear it, feel it or see it. It can be a suggestive sexual comment, it can be a touch, or an inappropriate photo or picture displayed in the workplace or in a classroom. The harasser may make sexual advances, initiating physical contact that is not wanted, display pornographic pictures, or make comments about another person's physical appearance. Sexual harassment involves unwanted, repeated sexual behavior or action toward another person. Sexual harassment creates a hostile work or academic environment that affects a person's ability to accomplish his or her objectives, either in the workplace or the classroom.

People who sexually harass others cannot claim ignorance, because this is a widely publicized issue. In addition, colleges provide printed copies of their sexual harassment policies and procedures to all faculty, staff and students. Eleven safety guides are listed to help you with sexual harassment in the workplace or academic environment.

11 Safety Guides on Sexual Harassment

Guide 1: Victims of sexual harassment find it emotionally unpleasant and frightening to take the step of reporting sexual harassment. Family and friends are the ones to rely on for emotional support.

Guide 2: The first step is to tell the harasser that his or her behavior is unwelcome and you want it to stop, you can do this verbally or in writing. Most people will get the message and stop. When the person stops the sexual harassing behavior without reprisal, chances are your message was well received and the problem is resolved. When the harassment continues after this warning, the following steps are necessary.

Guide 3: Take notes, take notes and take notes. Document when you told the person to stop sexually harassing you. Document his or her response. Document all incidents. Be specific about what the person is doing and saying that is sexually harassing. Your documentation of sexual harassment incidents should include times, dates, places. When pornographic photos, pictures or literature are involved, get a snap shot of the offensive material. Snapshots of the erotic or pornographic literature or pictures tacked on bulletin boards or displayed elsewhere in the workplace or academic setting can be used as evidence. On the back of the photo, write down the date, time, location and the name of the person taking the photo. Unless you have evidence, it is usually your word against his or her word. The more evidence, the better the chances of proving allegations of sexual harassment.

Guide 4: Report sexual harassment incidents to your supervisor or another higher authority. When the harassing person is a supervisor or professor, go to the next higher authority or another college official. Many colleges designate the department head as the person to whom you should report incidents of sexual harassment. The dean of students or his/her designee should be informed of incidents of sexual harassment.

Guide 5: Witness statements are important in proving sexual harassment. Write down the names of everyone who witnessed the sexual harassment. The investigator assigned to your case will need to interview all witnesses and obtain sworn testimony from them.

Guide 6: Has anyone else been victimized? Ask your classmates or coworkers whether this person has sexually harassed them. Has this person been accused of sexual harassment previously and have any prior investigations been conducted? Prior incidents or allegations show a pattern of sexual harassment by this person. This is important to know. People who sexually harass often have more than one victim.

Guide 7: No one should ever have to remain at the same work location or in the same classroom with a sexual harasser, especially during an active investigation. Physical proximity to this person can lead to intimidation and possible retaliation toward the complainant. Ask that either the harasser or you be assigned to another work area, or another supervisor. In an academic environment, reassignment to another class and instructor is a solution. Preferably the harasser is the one to be moved to an alternate area.

Guide 8: Any hostility, reprisal or mistreatment from the harasser or others should be reported to the department head and the dean of students.

Guide 9: When you are questioned about your allegations, the interview will usually be tape-recorded. Be honest, truthful, and as factual as possible. Being sexually harassed is not only humiliating but also emotionally straining and stressful. Do your best to control your emotions since they can impede your ability to be precise and factual. This is difficult!

Guide 10: While an investigation is active, it is confidential and is not made available to the public until the investigation is completed. Each state has it is own public records laws that dictate confidentially, and the release of the complainant's name. Ask the dean of students or the investigator to explain the public record law pertaining to sexual harassment complaints of that state.

Guide 11: Once the investigation is completed and the findings have been determined, ask for a copy of the investigation and findings. Retain a copy for your file.

Stop Sexual Harassment

Reporting or not reporting sexual harassment is a personal decision, and you will have individual reasons for either reporting or not reporting this form of abuse. Some people choose to endure a bad situation, some choose to remove themselves from the harassment and others report the incidents. Once you decide to move forward with your complaint - prepare, document and stand firm on your personal convictions. You may or may not get the results you want and expect. Allegations have to be proved or disproved. The more evidence you have to prove your allegations, the better your chances of proving the sexual harassment. One factor will remain from your report of sexual harassment: a paper trail is now established.

Chapter 12
DANGER! ALCOHOL AND DRUGS IN USE

Ask Yourself:
Do I drink too much and forget what I have done?

On-campus crime statistics for 1988 show liquor law violations reaching 25,818. In 1999 the number of liquor law violations escalated to 134,779. In November 1999, a junior died due to heavy drinking. In 1998, a 21-year-old sophomore died after consuming 24 shots of alcohol. Emergency incidents involving alcohol poisoning have also escalated. Alcohol is involved in 70 percent of murders and other crimes of violence. Sixty percent of sex offenders used alcohol when committing the offense. Drug abuse violations in 1998 reached 9,906 and climbed in 1999 to 28,948. The use of ecstasy and other designer drugs alarmingly continues to increase among teenagers, more than 1000 percent since 1995. In 2001, a 19-year-old died at a fraternity party due to a lethal dose of ecstasy. A 19-year-old student died at a fraternity house from ingesting OxyContin with alcohol. Drug use is dangerous and has proven to be fatal.

How Do I Communicate the Dangers to You?

How do I convince you to never drink too much alcohol or to stop using illegal drugs? How do I explain to you the reality that your life and possibly another life is at stake if you drink too much or use illegal drugs? How do I convey to you that the drug lords and drug peddlers do not care about the health and safety of you and your friends, or that their sole interest is only to profit from someone else's destruction? How do I communicate to you that a DUI or other arrests associated with alcohol or drugs affect your current and future endeavors? Convincing someone to put a halt to binge drinking or drug use is difficult, although the personal dangers that exist are critical to your success or failure while attending college and also afterwards.

Most of us know that alcohol and drugs are dangerous to health, safety and overall personal wellness. Why then do so many people use and abuse alcohol and drugs? Alcohol and drugs are used in many different cultures, by various age groups, by both men and women, and in many different socioeconomic circumstances. College students are not excluded and, in fact, are inclined to have higher rates of alcohol and drug use.

Why does a college life style influence students to use drugs and alcohol? Curiosity, socialization, stress, and peer pressure are all contributory factors. In 1998, Duke University conducted a study known as "The Duke Core Alcohol Survey." The survey identified reasons why Duke students consume alcohol. These reasons included socialization, relaxation, fun, to diminish personal shyness or to personally prove something. Some like the taste of an alcoholic beverage or feel a need to have a drink in their hand at parties.

The Number One Problem: ALCOHOL ABUSE

Alcohol is the number one depressant. Alcohol abuse is on the top of the list of behaviors that can and do affect educational goals and objectives. Not all college students abuse alcohol, but many do. Students who do not recognize the problems associated with alcohol abuse are more likely to become dependent on alcohol, sustain physical and mental damage, live unsafely and violate the law, conditions that can only result in substantial losses. Your health and safety, along with your dreams and aspirations are jeopardized when alcohol or drug use is part of your life.

The primary goal for you and most college students is getting a degree. A sure way to put a wedge into that goal is heavy drinking and lots of partying. Alcohol abuse places you in situations that could be avoided if you had a higher level of self-esteem and self-accountability for your decisions and behavior. Those who drink excessively, to the point where their minds and bodies are impaired, are more vulnerable to life-threatening situations such as rape, murder, hazing, suicide, vehicular accidents and falling from high places. People who drink too much are not able to think logically and cannot make good decisions about anything. Smart students acquire knowledge about alcohol use and abuse, become able to recognize individual tolerance, know the affects of alcohol, are responsible for their behavior and decisions, and understand how social influences affect a person's susceptibility to use or abuse alcohol.

Ask yourself some probing individual questions. Do I have or am I developing a dependence on alcohol? Is my health at risk because of my drinking habit? Do I drink too much and too often? Do I cut class or work because of a hangover? Are my grades suffering because of my partying and drinking habit? When drinking, do I experience periods of time that I can't remember (blackouts)? When I drink, do I make bad decisions and later feel embarrassed for my behavior? Have I had sex with someone I do not know, or cannot remember after drinking too much? Do I drink to get drunk? Am I experiencing personal relationship problems because of my drinking? Do my friends and family comment on how much I drink? Do I select friends who like to drink? If you answer "yes" to these questions it should raise a "red flag" that you are heading down the wrong road and need to change the direction of your path.

Duke University researchers developed a list of questions about drinking behaviors that can help you assess whether you have a potential drinking problem.

SSS Web reference:
http://www.mc.duke.edu/h-devil/drugs/at-duke.htm.

The questions are presented in separate categories to include academic success, family and relationships, peers, health, legal issues, financial issues and general concerns. Candid answers to these questions are necessary to accurately self-assess individual alcohol use.

According to the Ninth Special Report to the U. S. Congress on Alcohol and Health, environmental factors that contribute to alcohol use include cultural norms, the influence of family or friends and stressful life factors. It is important to ask yourself, am I developing an addiction? If your answer is yes, take the necessary steps to overcome the addiction and get back to the quality of life that you deserve. Most college campuses offer confidential counseling services or professional referrals to help students overcome alcohol and drug abuse. You may feel apprehensive about being judged or labeled as having a drinking problem. It is important to remember that we are human and there are times in our life when we fumble, make mistakes and are vulnerable, but we can learn from our mistakes and find the courage and determination to make necessary changes.

Binge Drinking

The Harvard School of Public Health defines binge drinking as the consumption of five or more drinks in a row for males, and four or more drinks in a row for females. The physical affects of alcohol are different from individual to individual. One person may be able to have three beers and not be intoxicated, whereas another person may have three beers and be intoxicated. The University of Illinois at Urbana-Champaign McKinley Health Center has identified several factors that determine how the amount of alcohol consumed will affect the body. These factors include how fast you drink, how much food is in your stomach, whether there are other chemicals in the beverage, your body weight, your individual tolerance to alcohol, how long you have been drinking, the environment, your expectations before drinking, your general physical and emotional health, gender difference, and whether you have taken other drugs.

How harmful is alcohol to your body? Overuse and long time use of alcohol causes structural and functional brain damage, and can cause hepatitis and cirrhosis of the liver. The Ninth Special Report to the U. S. Congress on Alcohol and Health summarizes it well, "Excessive alcohol use can cause widespread tissue and organ damage." Excellent educational videos about binge drinking called, "Wasted Youth" and "The Best Years of Your Life" are available through Security On Campus Inc. Their website information is found in Chapter 16, Resourceful Contacts.

SSS **W**eb reference: For more information about other drug and alcohol violations on college campuses, go to the web site for The Chronicle of Higher Education: http://www.chronical.com/free/v45/i38/38a00101.htm

Alcohol Related Arrests

How prevalent are arrests for alcohol violations on college campuses? According to an educational journal report, between 1997 and 1998 alcohol arrests increased 24 percent. According to a survey in the Chronicle of Higher Education, campus alcohol and drug arrests are rising. Since 1996, there has been a 10 percent increase in alcohol and drug arrests and a 5 percent increase in drug arrests on college campuses. As an example, a college in Michigan experienced their students involved in two riots where alcohol was a contributory factor and also resulted in 17 students being arrested. This is just one of many similar occurrences that happen on college campuses throughout the United States. Where there is alcohol, there is usually a fight. Men: A few intoxicated men have a higher probability of getting involved in a fight that can turn bad, resulting in serious injury or death.

DUI stands for driving under the influence. Indicators that standardize intoxication involve blood alcohol level or the breath alcohol level. Measuring blood alcohol level is the amount of alcohol the person has in their bloodstream. Breath alcohol level measures the amount of alcohol vapor a person has in their breath. When the driver is under the influence of alcoholic beverages or a substance that impairs a person's normal faculties, a person is subject to being charged with DUI. Penalties for the first DUI conviction include: a fine, imprisonment, probation, completing substance abuse course, and/or revocation of your driver license. Being without your auto will certainly change your ability to go where you need to go, and makes you dependent on others for transportation.

No one thinks about or means to seriously injure or kill another person because of the decision to drive while intoxicated. We have all heard the tragic stories, but never place ourselves in the driver's seat. Knowing that you injured or killed someone because of negligence and irresponsibility is something that will haunt you forever. According to the Ninth Special Report to the U. S. Congress on

Alcohol and Health, alcohol is a factor in approximately 44 percent of all fatal traffic crashes. According to this report, in 1993, 28 percent of all DUI fatalities involved drivers between the ages of 16 to 24. Solutions are to refrain from drinking and driving, and when you plan to drink, have a designated driver who is not drinking. There is no justification for putting yourself and others in jeopardy because of drinking and driving. No circumstances justify putting yourself at risk by riding with someone who is driving after drinking. One of the worst times for making a decision is when we drink alcohol, and ironically, people mistakenly think they are making good decisions when drunk.

When you plan to go out and drink, it is smart to know state and local alcohol laws and college rules and regulations applicable to drinking alcohol on campus and in the community. The college's student judicial system will impose penalties for alcohol violations, and campus and local police will enforce state laws and city ordinances relative to alcohol. Ignorance of the law will never constitute a valid excuse. The use of alcohol is a general public concern and there is "zero tolerance" for drinking and driving. No one can be lax or irresponsible about this issue. The consequences are too great, since you can end your life or take the life of another because of drinking and driving. This is inexcusable and totally preventable.

As mentioned before, when a safe ride is not available, call a taxi, a friend or a family member to come and get you. In my continual interactions with college students like you, many have told me they have a pre-arranged designated driver to pick them up and take them home after they have been drinking. I highly commend these students for their responsible decision to let a sober friend drive after they have been drinking alcoholic beverages.

All the news is not good. My communication with hundreds of college students has given me personal knowledge that an alarming number of college women choose to get into a car with a stranger after drinking, and night-clubbing. Drinking alcohol causes vulnerability and intoxication impairs one's ability to detect danger. Women: never allow yourself to consider accepting a ride with a stranger or giving a man you do not know or an acquaintance a ride home. Men: you are leaving yourself wide open to rape accusations when you pick up a woman you do not know, go to your place or her place and engage in sex when she is intoxicated or on drugs. Drinking alcohol or using drugs does hinder your ability to make good decisions. Help her find a safe passage home.

ILLEGAL DRUG USE

The freewheeling 1960s is known as the era of "sex, drugs and rock 'n roll." Since the 1960's, do you think drug use has increased or decreased? According to the National Household Survey on Drug Abuse, in 1962, four million U. S. citizens had tried an illegal drug. By 1999, 87.7 million had tried an illegal drug, an alarming increase. Drug use is also increasing among college students. In addition to illegal drugs impacting personal health, academic performance and overall well being, drugs contributes to violent crimes, less productive work environments, and a monetary loss of about $110 billion dollars a year to the U.S. economy. Choices and decisions college students make today influence your future and our country's future.

Dangerous & Life Threatening Drugs
Found on College Campuses

Illegal drugs are widely available in the United States. A wide array of drugs can be bought any time of the day or night and on many street corners. This is disheartening, but it is reality. Our neighbor to the south, Colombia, continues to be a global leader in producing and distributing cocaine. Mexico produces and illegally supplies the U.S. with impure heroine known as "black tar" that has a texture similar to tar used on roofs and is hard like coal. MDMA or "ecstasy" enters the U. S. from Europe through Israeli organized crime syndicates in conjunction with Western European traffickers. This global drug activity weakens our country and its citizens, causing vulnerability and distraction from other pressing concerns, locally and globally.

Illegal drugs tend to fall into three categories: depressants, stimulants, and hallucinogens. Depressants include alcohol, barbiturates, methaqualone, and benzodiazephines. The form can be liquid, powder and pill. Depressants affect speech and perception. An overdose can cause respiratory deficiencies, coma or death. Stimulants include caffeine, nicotine, phenmetrazine, methamphetamines, and amphetamines. Stimulants are harmful to the heart and respiratory system, increase blood pressure and cause a loss of appetite. Stimulants in a person's body cause moodiness and anxiety. Hallucinogens include LSD, mescaline, certain mushrooms, ecstasy, and marijuana. Hallucinogens may be in the form of a white powder, a liquid that can be injected into the body, a tablet or capsule that can be digested though eating, or plant material that can be eaten or smoked. A person's mental state is at risk when using hallucinogens, since these drugs can cause hallucinations and visual distortions, leading to both short-term and long-term damage. Users may experience behavior and mood alterations and can become violent and emotionally un-predictable with possible suicidal thoughts, anxiety and increased heart rate and blood pressure. Although marijuana is a relatively mild hallucinogen, it causes serious damage to the lungs and can cause other health problems that will be discussed below.

An array of narcotics and other drugs can be found among today's college students. Marijuana remains in common use, along with ecstasy, GHB, rohypnol, and other dangerous drugs. Since drugs are present in the college environment, and many students elect to try or use illicit drugs, you need to be able to identify all drugs you may encounter, know the health damage associated with each drug, and know the behaviors and mental states caused by each drug.

Marijuana continues to be a popular drug among the American population, including college students. Marijuana comes from the cannabis plant. Common derivatives of this plant include Sinsemilla, hashish and THC (delta-9-tetrahydrocannabinol). Cannabis is cultivated in isolated areas and in specially prepared indoor locations. Marijuana is primarily smoked like a cigarette, also referred to as a joint. Another tool for smoking marijuana is called a blunt, made by hollowing out a cigar and replacing the tobacco with cannabis. Marijuana users sustain red eyes, impaired motor skills, dry mouths, increases in heart rate, and hunger. Some users experience fantasies, paranoia or hallucinations. What does cannabis do to a person's health? Cancer is a possibility for marijuana users. Marijuana contains toxins, including cancer-causing chemicals that are stored in the users' fat cells for months. Similar to tobacco, smoking marijuana causes emphysema, bronchitis and bronchial asthma and may cause lung cancer. In other words, marijuana impairs your ability to breathe normally. Before lighting up the next marijuana cigarette, consider whether the "high" is more important than your lungs, your health and your longevity.

MDMA or ecstasy is not a new illegal drug on the market. A German company first developed this chemical mix in 1912 as a way to suppress the appetite. Ecstasy is comprised of chemical variants of stimulants, amphetamines or methamphetamines and hallucinogens. In the 1960s MDMA was popularly used and by the late 70s the drug was briefly associated with psychotherapy. It was not until the late 80s that MDMA was used in conjunction with other drugs, but alcohol was not a common mix at that time. In 2001, ecstasy became popular as a club drug, particularly at rave clubs or "The Scene" and other dance clubs. According to the Office of National Drug Control Policy (ONDCP), people between the ages of 18 and 25, college-age students, use ecstasy the most.

Ecstasy is a synthetic drug and comes in the form of a small pill or capsule. Once taken, the effects last for about 4 to 6 hours. Affects include feeling positive, empathetic, and relaxed. Some users feel anxiety. Ecstasy suppresses hunger, thirst and the desire to sleep, which means, it is not uncommon for users to participate in two-to-three day dance parties. Common sense tells us this leads to fatigue, dehydration, hypothermia, and can also lead to heart and kidney failure. The human body requires sleep and plenty of water to sustain good health. Health risks associated with ecstasy range anywhere from nausea to death. Symptoms include chills, sweating, teeth clenching, muscle cramps, blurred vision, high blood pressure, faintness, seizures, rise in body temperature, heart failure or stroke. Other affects to the body are liver damage, and serotonin-producing neuron damage that impacts the regulating of sleep, sexual activity, mood and aggression. In addition to these health hazards, the after affects can involve paranoia, depression and anxiety. According to researchers with the Johns Hopkins/National Institute of Mental Health (NIMH), MDMA/ecstasy users are susceptible to induced brain serotonin neurotoxicity that impairs the memory. MDMA also impairs a person's cognitive abilities, such as verbal reasoning, and the ability to be attentive for any length of time. How can anyone succeed as a college student if she or he cannot reason verbally, remember material, or pay attention for any length of time? Is ecstasy worth the risk to your physical and mental health? A four to six hour high is a heavy price to pay for both short-term and long-term damage. Before trying ecstasy or reusing the drug, ask yourself – is it really worth it?

Gamma Hydroxybutyrate or GHB was synthesized in the 1960s as a central nervous system depressant. GHB is a whitish colored powder that dissolves in water or alcohol. It comes in liquid form and is odorless and colorless. These qualities make it the ideal drug for rape predators to slip into a drink without the drinker's knowledge or consent. This is illegal and extremely dangerous. GHB was once available at health food stores as a body building additive. Since GHB is now an illegal drug, clandestine labs manufacture this drug and control, or fail to control, the level of purity of the drug, making this drug even more dangerous and unpredictable. GHB is commonly taken with alcohol. Like ecstasy, rohypnol and ketamine (special K), GHB is found at rave parties and other dance clubs and is used by rapists to sexually assault their victims without their knowledge or consent nor remembrance of what happened. A predator may carry GHB in a visine container or similar container that is designed to dispense liquid droplets into a drink. The potential for personal danger cannot be overstated, and criminal punishment for GHB use is severe. Less than 1 gram of GHB consumption causes muscle tone loss and reduces the user's inhibitions. Other affects include relaxation, a slower heart rate, slowed respiration, nausea, vomiting, depression, hallucinations, amnesia, seizures, depression, respiratory failure, loss of consciousness, coma and death. Depending on how much GHB is taken, the drug's effects can last from ten minutes to six hours long.

According to the Drug Abuse Warning Network and the Annual Emergency Room Data, the number of emergency room incidents related to GHB use in the United States has escalated drastically over the past decade. GHB is a dangerous and potentially fatal drug for college students and for society as a whole. Under no circumstances is this drug worth the risk.

Rohypnol, also known as "rophies" or the "date-rape drug" is similar to GHB. Royhypnol is a central nervous system depressant. Although prescribed as a sedative in Europe, it is an illegal drug in the United States and Canada. Rohypnol is a benzodiazepine, a sedative that is greater in potency than valium. In the United States, rohypnol was first recognized in 1993 as an illegal drug being used in south Florida. This drug often comes in the form of round white pills smaller than an aspirin. High school and college students are the predominant users of rohypnol, which is found at rave parties and similar dance club environments. Drug and alcohol addicts also use this drug to lessen their withdrawal symptoms. Heroin users find that rohypnol alleviates their heroin withdrawal. Rohypnol is taken either by snorting, by injection or orally. Rohypnol is also used in conjunction with alcohol or marijuana because of the enhanced intoxicating affect. It takes about 30 minutes to feel its affects and peaks about 2 hours later, then lingers up to eight hours. Manufacturers that illegally distribute this drug use bubble packaging to make the drug appear to be a non-threatening and harmless drug. These manufactures are depending on you to be vulnerable and unaware of the dangerous affects of the drug, as they laugh their way to the bank. The Hoffman-LaRoche Company, a legal manufacturer outside the United States, recognizes the problem of a colorless drug not being detected in liquid, so the company has developed a green colored tablet. The new tablet slowly dissolves in liquid. This may help to some degree, but it does not stop would-be rapists from dropping rohypnol into a drink that already has coloration to camouflage its presence. Counterfeit rohypnol pills are trafficked into the United States from Mexico.

What are the health risks associated with rohypnol? Harmful affects include impaired motor skills, lower blood pressure, drowsiness, amnesia, impaired memory, dizziness, nightmares and tremors. In the long run, the use of this drug can involve physical dependence and excruciating withdrawal. A rapist knows the drug's affects guarantee that their victim will have impaired judgment, become dizzy, black out, and not remember what happened. Rohypnol can also cause aggressive behavior. Even bartenders have been known to slip a date rape drug into a drink, so always watch the bartender prepare your drink.

Ritalin, a drug prescribed by doctors to treat ADHD, is a brand name for methylphenidate. Ritalin is a stimulant that has pharmacological affects similar to those of amphetamines and co-caine. College students acquire ritalin from friends or acquaintances who have access to a prescription. Ritalin comes in tablet form and is taken orally or snorted as a powder. Injection of this drug causes serious damage to a person's health because it blocks blood vessels, damages lungs, and has an effect on the eye's retina. Some college students use ritalin to study for longer periods of time because it increases attentiveness and focus on course materials. Others take ritalin as a diet pill, since it causes loss of appetite. Ritalin also induces an euphoric feeling, which can lead to serious psychological dependence on the drug. Ritalin use is known to increase heart rate and blood pressure.

OxyContin is an oral oxycondone (oxycondone hydrochloride), a time-released narcotic whose affects last up to 12 hours. Manufactured by Purdue Pharmaceutical, OxyContin comes in a tablet form in doses of 10, 20, 40 or 80 milligrams. This narcotic is prescribed to patients with severe pain. OxyContin, broken into a chewable or crushed form, is released and absorbed rapidly into the body. Side affects include severe hypertension, respiratory problems, nausea, sedation, vomiting, sweats, weakness, dizziness, and death. Oxy-Contin is an extremely addictive drug and only taken as prescribed by your doctor. OxyContin used in conjunction with alcohol is lethal.

OxyContin is obtained illegally by means of being stolen from pharmacies or purchased from people who have a prescription for it. Friends are giving friends this drug. Those who give this drug to others will go to prison. Unless this drug has been prescribed to you by a doctor and taken in whole tablet form, without any alcohol consumption, stay away from it.

Ketamine, also known as K or special K, is a drug used by veterinarians on animals. Ketamine has also been used as a general anesthetic on humans. Ketamine comes in the form of a white powder, similar to cocaine, and is dissolved in alcoholic beverages, smoked in conjunction with marijuana, or snorted. An increasing number of college students use ketamine, another dangerous drug found at rave parties. What are the health considerations? Ketamine causes sensory impairment, lack of coordination, impaired judgment and hallucinations. The affects last between 10 to 24 hours. It is smart to leave this drug where it belongs, in veterinary clinics for the medical needs of animals.

Phencyclidine (PCP) is a prescription drug and, like ketamine, is used in veterinary medicine. In the 1960s, PCP was used as a veterinary anesthetic and is now an illegal drug. Other names associated with PCP are killer weed, rocket fuel, angel dust, supergrass, and embalming fluid. These names clearly signify the dangers behind this drug, which has unstable affects. PCP is a white crystalline powder that dissolves in water. Like other drugs, such as heroin, contamination changes the white color to a darker color and gives it a gum-like texture. PCP is smoked after it is formed into a leaf-like material. Affects include slurred speech, lack of co-ordination, involuntary eye movement, auditory hallucinations, severe mood disorders, amnesia, distortion, acute anxiety, paranoia, and violent hostile behavior. PCP is a drug that brings nothing but danger and destruction.

Methamphetamine or meth is a central nervous system stimulant. This increasingly popular drug is a grave threat to our country's young people because of its lethal and unpredictable affects. Meth is also referred to as speed, crystal or ice. Meth is an odorless white powder that has a bitter taste when dissolved in water. Meth's crystalline structure resembles rock candy. The user smokes it like a cocaine user smokes crack. What are the health risks? Violent behavior can result from using meth. Meth increases heart rate, blood pressure, body temperature and respiration. Eye pupils become dilated and a feeling of euphoria occurs along with tremors and a boost in energy. Extensive use can result in paranoia, hallucinations, and violent erratic behavior. The Department of Justice describes "tweaking" as the time of greatest danger in the drug's cycle of use. Tweaking is when the abuser experiences drug-induced paranoia. The abuser does not sleep for three to fifteen days and becomes paranoid and petulant. The meth abuser experiences an increased craving, but no dosage recreates the euphoric high. During this stage, meth causes unpredictable behavior, which can include violent behavior. Choosing to use meth places you in a precarious, violent, hazardous and capricious situation. High doses can cause psychosis or death.

Cocaine is an extract from coca plant leaves indigenous to the South American Andean highlands. It is a white crystalline powder that is smoked, injected, inhaled or eaten. A heat-processed form of cocaine is known as "crack," a name derived from the crackling sound cocaine makes when it is heated. Crack comes in the form of crystalline rocks or slivers that are smoked in a pipe or inhaled as vapors. The health risks of cocaine include seizures, acute respiratory problems, heart failure, cerebral hemorrhaging, high blood pressure, insomnia, hallucinations, loss of appetite and death. Those who inject cocaine are susceptible to contacting HIV/AIDS. There is no antidote for an overdose of cocaine. According to the 1999 National Household Survey on Drug Abuse (NHSDA), 3.7 million Americans have used cocaine. Persons between the ages of 18 to 25 have the highest rate of cocaine use. Cocaine is dangerous and addictive.

Heroin is the processed form of opium, a juice extracted from poppy flowers. Heroin can be pure or impure. Pure heroin is a bitter-tasting white powder. The color of heroin is dependent on its purity. The darker the color the less pure it is. Dark heroin is known as "black tar". Heroin is snorted, smoked or injected.

Injecting heroin can lead to contracting HIV/AIDS or hepatitis. Heroin is an extremely dangerous and addictive drug. The health risks include drowsiness, respiratory depression, constriction of the eye's pupil and nausea. An overdose can result in a coma or death. Heroin use is on the rise, and so are fatalities from heroin use. According to the NHSDA, college students are in the age bracket that most commonly uses cocaine.

LSD is Lysergic Acid Diethylamide, a powerful hallucinogen synthesized in 1938 by Dr. Albert Hoffman. Dr. Hoffman found that lysergic acid diethylamide was a potent hallucinogen when he accidentally consumed the drug in 1943. This illicit drug was popular in the 1960s. Since then, the use of LSD has declined, although use showed an increase during the 1990s. LSD comes in a crystallized tablet form. LSD is also sold on sugar cubes and on squares of blotter paper. LSD comes from illegal labs in Northern California. How harmful is LSD to a person's health? This drug has serious long-term health affects, including flashbacks, anxiety and depression. LSD users experience dilated pupils, decreased body temperature, increased blood sugar levels, increased heart rate, and excessive perspiration. LSD causes a distorted sense of time, and also distorts the user's perceptions of shapes, movements, sounds, colors and sense of touch. The user's judgment and sense of danger are profoundly impaired, leading to an increased vulnerability to injuries. The affects of LSD can last from 10 to 12 hours and are referred to as a "trip."

Inhalants come in the form of aerosol sprays and nitrous oxide gas. A legal form of nitrous oxide is sold under the name of "whippets." Although whippets are legal, they are dangerous to your health. Inhalant use, sometimes called "huffing", is a dangerous practice that can result in a person becoming violent, disoriented and unconscious. The use of inhalants causes damage to the brain and central nervous system.

Anabolic steroids, sometimes used to enhance athletic performance, are dangerous. Health affects of steroids include aggression, depression, heart problems and liver cancer.

The active ingredient in tobacco is nicotine. It is usually smoked as a cigarette. Tobacco leaves can be chewed, and are more addictive than cigarettes. The affects include increased heart rate and high blood pressure. As we all know, tobacco causes cancer, emphysema and death.

Smart College Students Stay Clean and Clear of Alcohol & Drugs

Alcohol and drugs have been historically and still remain a dangerous activity associated with college life. Not all college students get caught up in alcohol consumption or drug use, but realistically, many college students binge drink and use harmful illegal drugs. Alcohol and drugs impair and debilitate a person both physically and mentally. A person's vulnerability to dangerous predators significantly increases when under the influence of drugs and/or alcohol. According to the U. S. Department of Justice, Drugs and Crime Data, drug users commit crimes more than nonusers. Many, if not most, prison inmates committed their offenses while under the influence of drugs and/or alcohol. Drugs and alcohol are enemies to personal wellness and safety.

Colleges throughout the United States offer students professional resources to help them overcome addictions. Attending alcohol and drug programs on campus will help you better understand alcohol and drug addiction and will introduce you to the resources available to help you with any drug or alcohol-related problems you may have. The ability to resist peer pressure and social activities that involve alcohol and drug use is important for your overall fitness, health and safety.

Recognize that membership in certain groups, such as fraternities, sororities, and all-male groups put you at greater risk for abusing alcohol and drugs. During the college assessment process, when deciding what college to attend, find out what resources are in place to reduce the influences of alcohol or drug use on campus and in the community. Here are some questions you need to ask: does the college have the reputation of being a "party" school? (Other students will have more knowledge about party activities.) How many deaths or serious injuries have occurred on campus that involved alcohol or drugs? Does the college provide students with educational programs about the abuse and other problems associated with drinking alcohol and using drugs? Are the college's alcohol and drug policies explained and enforced? Does the college offer crisis intervention, counseling or other professional referrals to help students with individual problems associated with alcohol or drugs? Does the college make students responsible for their actions and behaviors? Does the college encourage peer groups where students help other students? All these questions are important in your assessment of the college's commitment to alleviating problems associated with alcohol and drugs. The answers to these questions will help you assess your personal susceptibility to becoming involved in drug and alcohol use or to be victimized by those who do, on any particular campus. The use of alcohol and illegal drugs continues to inflict damage and destruction on college students, communities and our country. Knowing the affects and consequences of using illegal drugs and alcohol, and opting to never use or stop using drugs and/or alcohol, will make going to college a happier, more enjoyable and safer experience.

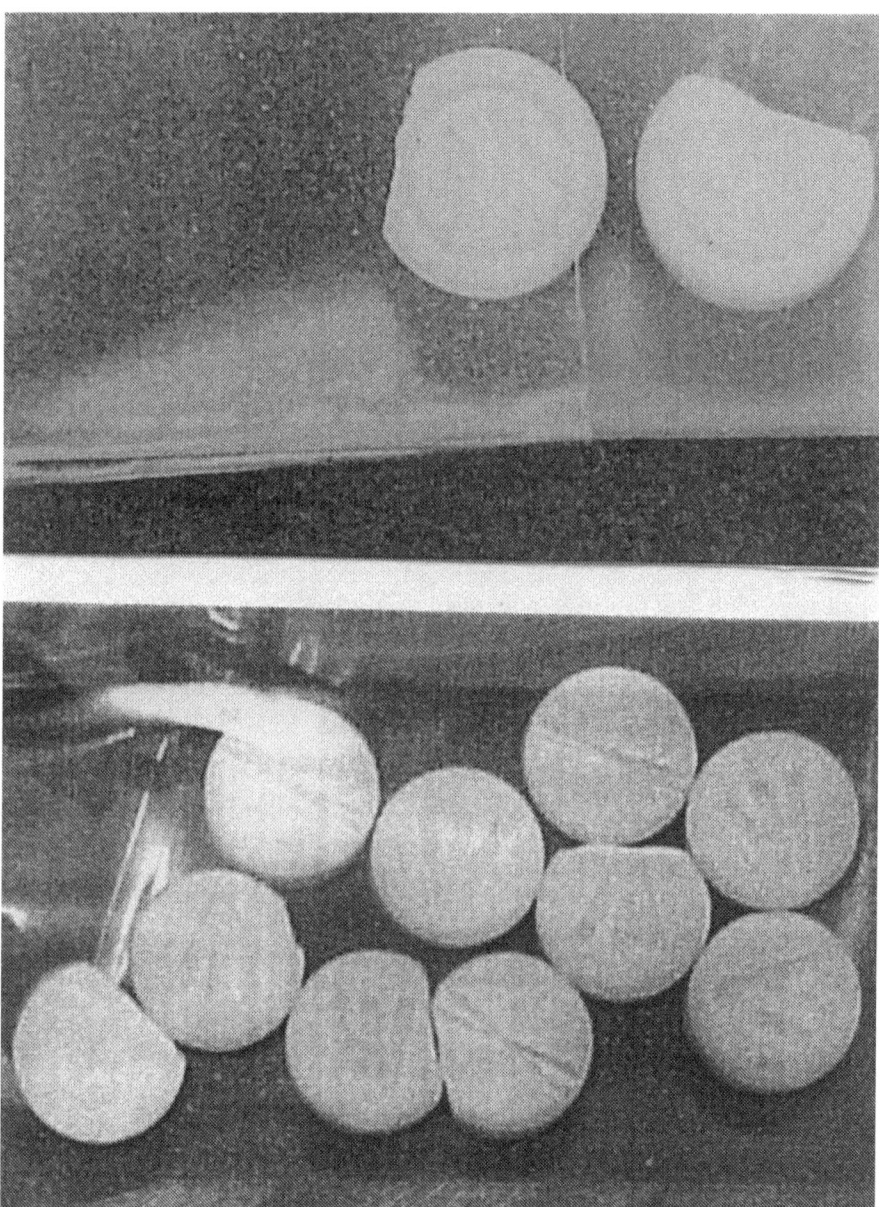

MDMA, ecstasy is a dangerous and life threatening date rape drug. Commonly found at Rave clubs

NATURAL SPRING WATER
5L /(1 PT, .9 FL OZ) /16.9 FL OZ

Date rape drug GHB is often times camouflaged in water bottles. GHB is a whitish powder and can easily be dissolved into a drink, undetected. MDMA or ecstasy is a synthetic drug resembling an aspirin tablet. Katamine, also known as "k" or "special k" is a drug that veterinarians use on animals.

Chapter 13
STUDENT HOMICIDE

Ask Yourself:
Have I ever left a party
with someone I did not know?

The thought of any college student being murdered is inconceivable, but tragically, reality has demonstrated to us that young people are victims of homicide. The death of Jeanne Clery, the long trail of college women killed by Ted Bundy, and Danny Rolling's heinous murders of five college students are painful reminders of the reality of college students murdered. Criminal homicide includes murder and manslaughter. The U. S. Department of Education's Report to Congress, January 2001, lists 11 murders committed on-campus in 1999. Of the 11, three were committed in residence halls.

To best safeguard yourself against dangerous predators it is vitally important to master key personal safety guides and apply these guides to your daily life. After reviewing a few homicide incidents that involved college students, you will be able to analyze how predators access an opportunity to murder and then highlight some key safety factors that can help you be a safer person.

Primarily other college students and non-students within their own age group are the culprits that victimize college students. Two of the most notorious, heinous murderers of college students, causing excruciating pain and suffering to students, families, college and community, were serial killers, Ted Bundy and Danny Rolling. A closer look into the opportunities Bundy and Rolling sought out to target and murder their victims will help you assess your own behaviors and deter criminal victimization.

THE KILLER'S WINDOW OF OPPORTUNITY

Serial killer Ted Bundy

Theodore Bundy, one of the most arrogant and cold-hearted killers in U.S. history, appeared to be a handsome, charming law student and political activist. He had the ability to mask his real personality and abnormal behaviors from his victims and also the people that knew him. Did Ted Bundy look for opportunities to commit murder? Absolutely, yes! According to an interview that Stephen G. Michaud had with Bundy, *"opportunity"* was a key factor that Bundy looked for before carrying out his crimes.

Opportunity to Commit the Crime

A woman fumbles with her car keys. She is inattentive when she walks toward the parking lot to her car. The predator is waiting for her, as he holds an object to strike her with. He strikes her. She falls to the ground and screams. He panics and runs.

Prevent Criminal Intrusion

How can this be avoided from happening to you? First of all, do not park your vehicle in an isolated area; secondly, have your keys positioned in your hand to readily access your vehicle; thirdly, know who and what is around you; and lastly, screaming to draw attention can be an effective response to scare off your assailant.

Opportunity to Commit the Crime

A young college woman disappears from her bedroom one evening. She is later found dead by police in an isolated, wooded area. The killer, prior to killing her, familiarized himself with her house without her knowing of his presence. Easy access into the house where the doors and windows were commonly left unlocked allowed her killer to silently enter the house and room late at night. *This is the window of opportunity for the killer.*

Prevent Criminal Intrusion

How do we avoid this from happening to you? If you see a suspicious person or vehicle around your house or apartment, call the local or campus police department (depending on jurisdictional boundaries) with a description of the person and/or vehicle. The most significant lesson here is *always secure doors and windows with a good locking system and a security alarm.* Easy access into a home, apartment or room opens the door to criminal opportunity.

Opportunity To Commit the Crime

A woman sits alone in a library. She appears to be depressed and lonely. A man sitting nearby her is intuitive to her mood and sits beside her and starts a friendly conversation. She assumes he is another student when he asks her to go out with him for a drink and something to eat. She leaves with him and also gets into his car. He brings her to an isolated area and raped and killed her.

Prevent Criminal Intrusion

How do you avoid this happening to you? The lesson to learn here is *not to appear needy or vulnerable when you are out in public.* Head down, shoulders slumped, sad and searching face – these are behaviors that let others know you are depressed and lonely and maybe a little desperate. The more vulnerable you look, the more confident the criminal is that he can successfully approach you. The most significant lesson from this tragedy is *do not allow anyone you do not personally know to get too close and friendly with you.* The time of greatest danger is when she left with this strange man and got into his car. Many college women do leave parties with a man they just met, or accept a ride home from someone unknown to them. This is an extremely dangerous practice. I cannot emphasize this enough: *Do not leave with a new acquaintance or stranger. It is this simple - do not get into his car.*

Have you noticed how open people are to help others in time of need? Knowing this, predators, such as Bundy, may set up a phony situation to solicit help from a woman. One of Bundy's tactics involved posing to have a broken arm held in a sling and then asking a woman to help him get into his car. Be cognizant of these types of predator tactics. You can help from a distance by making a phone call for the person. Think of your safety first.

Opportunity to Commit the Crime

Another college woman was strangled and later found in an isolated area. She was hitchhiking when he picked her up and invited her to go to a party with him. Since she had no plans at the time, she accepted. He took her to his home, got her drunk, raped her, and then killed her by strangling her to death.

Prevent Criminal Intrusion

How do you avoid this from happening to you? Hitchhiking alone or with another person is dangerous and you should never get to your destination by hitching a ride. A safety conscious person never gets into someone's vehicle that they do not know. Once you get inside a vehicle with an unknown person, you immediately hand over personal power and control to this stranger. Remember, *always maintain personal power and control for your own protection and never release it to anyone else.* Losing your ability to take care of yourself because you are under the influence of alcohol and/or drugs creates another significant danger. Using drugs and/or alcohol can lead to the most dangerous situations that you can ever put yourself in. Your ability to know what is happening around you, who is around you and what others are doing is critical for your personal safety.

Serial killer Danny Rolling

It is August 1990, and a fresh, new school year is underway. Thousands of college students are settling into their new community.

The community is humming with thousands of students moving into their new residents, shopping, eating at restaurants and enjoying community theaters and nightclubs. Students, either beginning college for the first time or returning to college for another semester, light up their community with liveliness and excitement. New students soon realize that they are not alone in being strangers in this heavily congested college environment. Anticipation, excitement, uncertainty and confusion are all in the air.

One of the most heinous, torturous serial killers in history, Danny Rolling, selected this time and these circumstances to take the lives of five college students in August 1990. Rolling mingled in the community along with the students, undetected, causing no alarm by his presence. These students were preparing to enjoy their college life, until Rolling torturously murdered them.

The two main points to remember are; *always be aware that you are a stranger in a new environment*; and *realize that moving to a new place alters your lifestyle from what you are accustomed to*. Family, friends and other known community members are not with you to protect and shelter you from the evil behaviors of others. When you leave home and go away to college, you have to become personally responsible and mature about your personal safety.

The Killer's Path

Never let anyone get in a position to take your power and control away from you. Your personal safety can never be compromised and you can never be indolent about it. You have to be shrewd, attentive, suspicious and aware of what and who is around you. I am not advocating that you live in a state of constant fear and paranoia but be wary of people you do not know, including other students. Use your mind, body, intuition, instincts and safety skills to be an unattractive and inconvenient target for a criminal. Being safety smart includes learning, developing, applying and practicing safety smart guides, and acquiring personal safety skills and techniques through education, repetition and practice.

Criminal opportunists repetitively visualize their crimes, and may have committed the same kind of crime before. Predators educate themselves on how to masterfully assess opportunity and select their victims. This killer presumably noticed one of his victims when he saw her shopping in a nearby convenience store, not far from his campsite in a nearby wooded area. The young woman lived alone in an attached home in a quiet neighborhood down the road from the store and not far from where the killer camped. Rolling later entered her home through an accessible sliding glass door in the back of her home. The back yard had a privacy fence that offered him privacy to break into her home without detection. When he entered her home, he tortured and killed her.

Serial killer, Danny Rolling camped out in these woods that are fenced from intruders. One of his victims lived down the road from the campsite where he clandestinely stayed. It is possible the killer saw his victim in a nearby neighborhood convenient store that they are both known to have shopped.

The Power of Self-confidence

It is essentially important to always safeguard yourself and to be suspicious of another person's actions, especially if he or she is too friendly, follows you, or stares at you. As discussed above, Bundy got close to his targeted victims by being friendly, befriending them, or by asking for their help. Criminals assess a person's vulnerability and their state of mind for depression, loneliness or insecurity and also evaluate their self-confidence, strength, level of awareness and their safety practices. *Be a powerful person by developing powerful safety skills and attitudes. Be confident, aware and alert.* Know what and who is around you. Never let strangers get too close or friendly with you. Maintain a straight posture where you keep your head up, back and shoulders straight, firm, and walk up-right, not slouched. This will reflect your self-confidence and inner-strength. The criminal does not like these positive personal attributes about you. He would rather seek out and prey on someone else who seems weak and vulnerable. You do not have to be a body-builder or athlete to reflect a strong sense of self. Presenting yourself as self-confident and safety smart will support your ongoing efforts to protect yourself against the criminals who lurk on college campuses and communities.

Precautionary Safety Smart Lessons to Learn

It is necessary to practice safety conscious skills. When you always know what and who is around you, you have a powerful advantage over a predator. If strangers or casual acquaintances come up to you when you are walking, at the beach, in a bar or restaurant, or other social settings, be wary, especially if the stranger acts too friendly. Question such a person's motives. For example, if a stranger comes up to you and pets your dog or cat, or starts small talk to get acquainted with you, this behavior should send up a red flag. I am not suggesting that every stranger who talks to you is a dangerous person, but how do you know who is safe and who is not? You do not know. The best personal safety practice is to be cautious, hard to approach, and hard to get to know. In the movie "Oxygen," a young man approaches a middle-aged woman who is taking her dog out for her predictable, daily walk. The man knows this routine because he has had her under surveillance for weeks. The man approaches the woman with a smile. He immediately starts complimenting her on what a nice dog she has and even produces a doggie treat for the little dog. (Isn't that a big red flag!) She does not realize or sense any danger from this man and engages in friendly small talk with him. He manages to get closer to her. She is not aware that an unfamiliar car is parked nearby, with another man sitting in the driver's seat. What happens to the woman in this drama? She is kidnapped and buried alive. *Remember what your parents have constantly told you since you were a child, "do not talk to strangers."*

Chapter 14
THE DANGERS OF HAZING ACTIVITIES

Ask Yourself:
Do I know how to avoid being involved in hazing activities?

What is hazing? The word, "haze" is defined in Webster Dictionary as, "a. to harass by exacting unnecessary or disagreeable work, b: to harass by banter, ridicule, or criticism 2: to haze by way of initiation [such as] fraternity pledg[ing]." Have you been involved in or a victim of hazing? Hazing activities are more common among certain groups such as athletic groups, college fraternities and sororities, and military groups. Individuals involved in hazing activities usually do not anticipate negative results from their deviant actions or realize how their participation in hazing can end up being life-threatening or causing someone else's death. Contrary to popular belief, hazing is a life-threatening practice that can and has resulted in fatalities, regardless of intent. Before you decide to participate in hazing activities or allow others to pressure you into becoming involved in unnecessary and harmful situations, knowledge of the personal consequences, along with the criminal and civil litigation that follow, should deter you. Participation in hazing activities can strip away all the dreams and goals you have set for your future. You have made the decision to attend college for your personal and professional growth. You will need the maturity to maintain a steadfast, inner strength, refusing to let others take advantage of you because you want to be a member of a certain fraternity, sorority or athletic group. Your desire to belong may be an important personal goal that you thought about for a long time before

168

college. These strong feelings can make you vulnerable to obeying group members who tell you that you have to participate in hazing rituals or you can forget about your opportunity to join the group. Veteran members may try to manipulate or persuade you into doing things that are wrong and dangerous, activities you would never consider otherwise. Your responsibility is to safeguard yourself and your personal safety, which includes stopping others from placing you in dangerous and wrongful situations. Putting yourself above those who want you to participate in bad and harmful actions and not allowing others to persuade you to jeopardize your life and the lives of others, empowers you, not them. Hopefully, you will never allow anyone to take away your dreams or defeat your goals.

In reading some true hazing incidents, focus on how hazing activities deprived them of their goals and aspirations. Everyone loses with the game of hazing.

Ensuring your personal safety involves personal empowerment, being smart, and taking responsibility for your decisions. Never turn over your personal power to protect yourself to anyone. Demand and expect from others that they always treat you fairly and with respect. Less than that should never be acceptable to you. A consistent practice of never giving anyone power over you to place you in any unsafe situation is one of the smartest decisions you will ever make. You have the ultimate power to decide whether others will be allowed to influence you or put you in precarious situations. Your inner-strength and intelligence in avoiding these situations can also influence someone else to refuse to become a victim of mistreatment, cruelty, or serious harm.

True Hazing Stories

Hazing is not something that we normally think about or become involved with unless; one, we hear about a tragic story that involves hazing activity or; two, we participate actively, either voluntarily or involuntarily. Consequences can be emotionally and physically devastating to the hazing victims and their families. The following true stories are intended to show you the harm in hazing.

In March 2000, a college student was killed due to a car crash coupled with a fraternity initiation prank. The young man was handcuffed to a tree and blindfolded, when a vehicle crashed into the tree. Those involved in this hazing incident did not mean for the young man to die, but he did.

In November 1998, a sophomore was involved in an initiation into the college's marching band. He sustained a serious beating, mostly done by females using paddles.

In December 1997, hazing activities injured another student. His ankle was broken when he fell during an affray in a campus parking lot. It is reported that he was an innocent bystander when a vehicle driven by one of the fraternity participants in an attempted kidnapping prank nearly ran over him. The person who was being kidnapped was found bound with tape in the back of the vehicle. The young man's injuries resulted in permanent physical disability.

Anti-Hazing Statutes

Forty-one states have anti-hazing laws. In addition, states are taking further steps to stop hazing, by enacting tougher legislation and harsher penalties. Anti-hazing laws vary from state to state. For example, Alabama classifies hazing as a Class C misdemeanor. In Indiana hazing is a Class B misdemeanor or a Class C or D felony, depending the level of recklessness, injury and whether a weapon was involved. In Florida, hazing violations involve fines, withholding diplomas or transcripts, probation, college suspension or dismissal. In Georgia hazing is a misdemeanor of a high and aggravated nature. In Virginia, hazing which results in injury is a felony.

SSS Web reference: To find out about your state's hazing law refer to, www.stophazing.org.

The Alfred University Hazing Study

New York State's Alfred University conducted a study in 1999 on hazing that included the participation of athletes, coaches and staff personnel affiliated with the National Collegiate Athletic Association institutions. Alfred University's researchers defined hazing as, "an action that humiliates, degrades, abuses, or endangers, regardless of a person's willingness to participate." The study showed that hazing is gender neutral, involving both male and female athletes, although males are at a greater risk. Criminal activity and alcohol are involved in many hazing cases. According to the survey, "more than 250,000 people experienced some form of hazing to join a college athletic team." The national survey showed that 250,000 or more college athletes were involved in hazing in joining a college athletic group. Hazing activities that are illegal include putting people in restraints, beatings, kidnapping, destruction of property, and similar types of illegal activities. The study showed that one in five athletes were subjected to illegal hazing. Fifty percent of hazing activities involved the consumption of alcohol. Half of the hazing incidents involved alcohol-related hazing, such as drinking contests. Sixty-six percent of hazing incidents involved yelling, scaring, embarrassing and humiliating the hazing participants.

SSS Web reference: Alfred University's National Study on Hazing can be found at, http://www.alfred.edu.

Stay Away from Hazing Activities

Before joining a group of people who may recklessly endanger you and others, think about several safety smart factors. Find out about the group's past history and reputation before you make a commitment to join any group. Find out about the members, how they behave, and their level of involvement in the community. Ask probing questions. What is the reputation of the group in the college and local community? Does this group have a history of serious conduct violations, and what are the violations? You can find out about criminal and/or rule violation incidents by checking with the campus police department, the dean of students' office, or the campus life office. Talk with other students and current members of the group. Find out about their group values and what their expectations are of you. Write down the pros and cons of joining the group. Determine what you can expect from the group in comparison to what they expect from you. Determine whether or not the group is acceptable to you. The more you know about the group, the better able you are to determine its suitability for you as an individual. When hazing is a practice of the group you are considering, this should tell you that they are not acceptable to you.

Chapter 15
PERSONAL SAFETY & THE INTERNET

Ask Yourself:
Do I tell a lot about myself when I communicate on the Internet?

Internet global communication capacity allows us to communicate with friends and it also opens the opportunity to meet new friends. College students rely on their computers for research and communication, such as, instant messenger, email, chat room, web sites, news groups, etc. Using the Internet requires you to protect your privacy and keep yourself safe from computer cons or predators. Accessing information has never been easier, to include your personal information. The Internet makes it easy for anyone to access names, phone numbers, home addresses, working phone and address, credit card numbers, and so on. Predators have a keen sense in being able to hunt down others personal information through the Internet. More times than not, when you share personal information with a dangerous predator, you are not aware of the information you are providing to this person. How private and safe are you when communicating with others on the Internet? A golden rule to abide by is to not give out personal information that you do not want everyone to know. Communicating through chat rooms, email and other Internet friendly passages does not secure your privacy. Predators travel the highways and byways of the Internet seeking their prey. Their boundaries, at one time more limiting, are now broadened to include Internet users who do not protect their identity or communicate with others in a safety conscious manner. Pedophiles and other predators connect with new prospects over the Internet by learning their names, addresses, and details of their life like where they go to school, what teams they play on, etc. The Internet gives sexual predators and other criminals new ways to stalk and target people with the intent to commit a crime. When you communicate with total strangers, how do you know the information they give you about themselves is true? You may think you are talking to an 18-year-old man but the person might be a 50-year-old man with a criminal record. Before you decide to share personal information about yourself, or your family and friends, and before you develop a friendship, and agree to meet or date someone you do not personally know, there are serious safety considerations you need to assess and practice.

A college female student was using the Internet to communicate with a male student who attended college somewhere else. He was oblivious to the con game she was playing with him. The woman did not give out her real name, and she was not truthful about what she looked like. She emailed a photograph she claimed to be her, but it was her friend instead. This young man was not only naïve, but did not know how to protect his personal safety and identify. He gave the woman his full name, address and home phone number. The more trusting the man became, the more bogus the woman became. He spent many hours that year communicating with this woman who was, in reality, someone entirely different than the person she presented herself to be. When he was later informed about her scam, he was bewildered and confused. A personal safety guide to remember: *Do not send personal information or photos to a stranger you meet on the Internet.* How trusting are you going to be with someone unknown to you? The results of trusting a stranger on the Internet can be much more serious than they were in this case.

A True Story about Meeting Someone on the Internet

A freshman attending a college in Texas traveled to Austin one weekend and later was found dead from a gunshot wound to the head. His death resulted from the orchestration by a 31-year-old man from San Antonio during his numerous Internet communications with him. The 31-year-old man led this college student to believe that he was communicating with a female named Kelly. Since their email communication was going so well, they decided they would meet in

Austin. The young man was anxious and excited to finally meet this nice young woman named Kelly. He did not know that Kelly would turn out to be a 31-year-old man who would end his life. This college student never experienced another day, and never to return to college. Instead his life ended at the hands of a dangerous predator who used the Internet to portray himself as someone else. This was a preventable tragedy.

Many interesting and enjoyable communications go on between known and unknown persons where encountering danger seems unlikely. With a greater opportunity to communicate with other people and groups - locally, nationally, and internationally - it is essential that personal safety be a factor in all your communications and in all relationships developed over the Internet. When communicating with people you do not know, being safety conscious requires being wary of what people say or imply is true about them. Websites are provided to access more information about dating people you meet on the Internet.

SSS **W**eb reference: http://www.saferdating.com is an informative web site that discusses Internet dating in more detail.

SSS **W**eb reference: http://www.safeteens.com.

It is not to be implied that all Internet meetings and all relationships developed on the Internet turn out badly. Successful dating from Internet meetings does happen. The point is for you to be skeptical and cautious as you venture out onto the electronic highway. Here is another true story of deception and deceit.

Another True Story about Internet Dating

A young woman met a man through a chat room. The more common interests shared, the greater the Internet relationship flourished. After a month of interesting chat with each other, they decided to meet in a quaint mountain town. The first encounter turned out to be a wonderful experience in which her new friend was a gentleman. This reinforced her thoughts of how wonderful he was and how much they had in common. After a short period of time, the two decided to make their relationship more permanent. The woman quit her job and said her goodbyes to family and friends. She arrived at her new boyfriend's home and he kindly helped her get settled in. Shortly afterwards, his behavior toward her began to change. His attentiveness, consideration and care swiftly diminished. He began accusing her of lying to him, and listened in on her phone conversations. He became cold and distant. She went into debt paying for many of the household necessities. When she decided to leave him, he blamed her for the problems in the relationship. As a survivor of an abusive relationship, this woman warns others to be careful when dating through the Internet, not to trust so easily, and to know the person well before you get yourself involved.

The Risk in Telling Others About You

People like to talk about themselves, tell others about their interests, where they attend college, and what they are studying in college. It is okay to say that you are studying engineering or that you like to surf or ski. Refrain from sharing your telephone number, where you live, what college you attend, where you work and other personal information that could be used to track you down. The more you tell others about yourself, the more you expose yourself to a person or persons who might be assessing you as a possible target of criminal opportunity. Remember our story about the college student who was looking forward to meeting his Internet friend Kelly, but never considered his personal safety when deciding to meet someone he had never met in person or to question the authenticity and validity of this person. Being safety astute involves preventing opportunities for personal harm by being less trusting and more cautious about establishing any relationship with some one you do not know. You are more vulnerable when you travel to an unfamiliar place to meet someone. This opens the opportunity for a dangerous predator to fulfill his or her primary purpose in meeting you. I share this story with you as a reality about what does happen, and to emphasize that you must always practice personal safety in your communications and interactions with others, including on the Internet.

Ask yourself these questions. How often have you given out your name, home address, where you work or attend college, contact phone numbers, personal photos, and other personal information to people you know only through the Internet? How many of you, at one time or another, believed most of the information a person was giving you in emails? Some of us will acknowledge that we have made ourselves available to an Internet predator at one time or another. Taking a step back and assessing how much information we have given out to unknowns can lead to a discomforting concern for personal safety.

Predators also use the Internet as their tool to meet people. All different kinds of people, both good and bad, use the Internet to communicate and seek information. The more you make yourself known and the more receptive and open you are to meeting and dating people you do not personally know, the greater the opportunity for personal danger. The fallacy that victimization happens to others and not you applies here too. Chances are you will not become a victim, but you can enhance those odds to a lower chance of probability by giving predators no opportunity to know who you are or to take advantage of you.

How you represent yourself in your Internet communications gives others a perception about you. Others will determine your character by the computer name you give yourself, and/or the news groups or chat rooms you get involved with. All these factors paint a visual picture to others about your personality, vulnerabilities, strengths, weaknesses and the possibility that you will be receptive to promiscuous sexual activity. Referring to oneself as "Hot Pants," "Sexy," or "Lonely," and "looking for love" sends a message to others that you are probably looking for a sexual relationship and are open to promiscuity. The news groups and subject sites you choose to participate in, and the threads that develop from these subject sites expose you to people who may be specifically looking for people open to promiscuous sexual activity, or available for a personal meeting.

To illustrate this, I searched news groups and retrieved web sites that are specifically set up for people interested in deviant behaviors and promiscuous opportunities. Chat rooms on such sites provide information such as the author of the message, the respondents, and the subjects that are correlated with the authors. Although this might seem innocent and non-threatening to you, predators and pedophiles will seek out certain subjects and author names to target as possible victims of a future crime. Predators wander the thousands of pornographic sites available on the web. According to a Carnegie Mellon study, the extensive pornography found online includes sexual pictures, stories, film clips and descriptions. The pornography includes nudity, bondage, sadomasochism, defecation, and sex acts with animals. As an adult, your individual choice dictates if this material is acceptable or not acceptable to you on the Internet. Child pornography is never acceptable, and is illegal.

In short, be aware of the dangers and opportunities you expose yourself to when you are providing personal information to people you do not know or accepting an invitation to meet someone before you find out more about the person. Have a suspicious mind and avoid taking others at face value. If you do decide to meet someone from a chat room or email list, your innate common sense should caution you to avoid meeting this person in an unsafe and isolated area or situation. Only meet under controlled and safe circumstances. Communicating with a person on the Internet for an extended period of time can cause a person to let their guard down, begin to trust the person, and start considering a meeting with the person. Your personal safety skills and the need to maintain your personal power over the situation should override the inclination to meet someone you do not really know under compromising circumstances. Some people do form true friendships and love relationships with persons met online. If your Internet correspondent is a person of integrity, he or she will not mind being checked out before any meeting. Meet during the day in a public location that offers good visibility, and inform a friend or family member about the public meeting, including everything that you know about this person. Preferably, have a friend or family member accompany you to the meeting place. Also consider that an unknown person who is violent and dangerous can harm you and the person with you. Do not take short cuts in personal safety just because you have a friend with you.

What do you do when you are alone, waiting for your new Internet friend, and he shows up with a couple of buddies? Your instincts should tell you to get out of there as quickly as possible. Again, under no circumstance or conditions should you ever get into a vehicle with any person you do not know. Even if the first meeting is successful and non-threatening, continue these personal safety guides until you have learned more about this person to where you feel confident that the person is safe and does not pose a personal threat to you. This involves being curious and suspicious about the person's background history, life style, friends, work, and social groups. Do not assume the person is telling you the truth.

Protect Your Privacy

How easy is it for a predator or stalker to obtain your personal information or track you down? Easy! A name and telephone number published in the phone book provides an easy way to trace someone through web site http://www.anywho.com. Information given on this site includes not only your phone number and home address; it also provides a detailed map on how to get to your home. This site also lists your neighbors who have their names published in the telephone book. Be aware that if you give your real name in a chat room, a predator can find out a lot more about you. Here are nine personal safety guides to assist you when using the Internet.

9 Safety Smart Guides in Using the Internet

Guide 1: Avoid giving out your home phone number and where you live to people you do not know or have become acquainted with through the Internet. Avoid telling others too much about yourself.

Guide 2: Avoid calling collect to acquaintances you meet on the Internet. The person receives the phone number you used on his or her phone bill.

Guide 3: Use a Caller ID blocking device to block out your phone number.

Guide 4: Avoid putting your photo on the Internet, especially in a personal ad section.

Guide 5: Sharing information about where you attend college lets an unknown person know where to find you.

Guide 6: Select a computer name that is free of sexual connotations.

Guide 7: Select your web sites wisely before taking part in chat rooms or news groups.

Guide 8: Stay away from pornographic and obscene web sites. Obscenity and pornography, including child pornography, are commonplace on the web. These sites are nesting grounds for predators, pedophiles, rapists, and stalkers.

Guide 9: Report threatening or harassing Internet communications to the police.

Chapter 16
RESOURCEFUL CONTACTS

Ask Yourself: Do I know where to find help?

WHERE TO FIND HELP

Most of us do not know, in advance, how to deal with the aftermath of rape and other violent crimes, or how to extricate ourselves from domestic violence. After the fact, we find ourselves searching for help, and that is not the ideal time to be carrying out such a search. In the pages that follow you will find a list of victim service organizations at the local, state and federal levels, in addition to non-profit and private organizations. The organizations listed offer exceptional services; and also can refer you to the closest victim services locations. In addition, campus police, student services and your local police department are available to help you and connect you with the nearest victim services organization or crisis center. The local telephone book also provides victim services telephone numbers for your community, along with a separate section for local and state government agencies. Another resource is the Internet where there are web sites for U. S. Rape Crisis Centers, Domestic Violence Centers, and other similar resources. Security On Campus, Inc. has an informative web site for college students where names and locations of statewide victim assistance organizations can be found.

SSS Web reference: Security On Campus can be found at: http://campussafety.org/resources/victimassistance.

A note of caution about using the Internet when you are living with an abusive partner; he may check your Internet activity to find out who you are communicating with. Completely delete any sites and emails that you do not want your partner to find. Deleting sites usually requires deleting more than one function on your computer. If you are not certain that this information was deleted, contact the Internet provider and inquire about how to completely delete email and web site locations. You can also use a trusted friend's computer or the computer at the public library to find victim assistance organizations.

The following list of resources includes state and national organizations that help victims of violent crimes, such as domestic violence and sexual assault. In addition to the state and national phone numbers, a fraud resource information section is included, along with other helpful resources. Also included is a listing of web sites referenced in the safety smart chapters. These web sites are listed at the end of the resource list.

This list does not include all the services available, but is a primary resource list that can either directly assist you or refer you to the best resource for your situation. Know that you are not alone, and that help is near you.

LIST OF RESOURCES BY STATE

ALABAMA

Alabama Coalition Against Domestic Violence
Montgomery, AL, Phone: 334-832-4842
Toll free: 800-650-6522

Alabama Coalition Against Rape
Montgomery, AL, Phone: 334-264-0123

ALASKA

Alaska Network on Domestic Violence and Sexual Assault
Juneau, AK, Phone: 907-586-3650

ARIZONA

Arizona Coalition Against Domestic Violence
Phoenix, AZ, Phone: 602-279-2900

Arizona Sexual Assault Network (AzSAN)
Phoenix, AZ, Phone: 602-258-1195

ARKANSAS

Arkansas Coalition Against Domestic Violence
North Little Rock, AZ, Phone: 501-339-9486

Arkansas Coalition Against Sexual Assault
Harrison, AR, Phone: 870-741-1328

CALIFORNIA

California Alliance Against Domestic Violence
Modesto, CA, Phone: 209-524-1888

California Coalition Against Sexual Assault (CALCASA)
Oakland, CA, Phone: 510-839-8825

California Coalition for Battered Women
Long Beach, CA, Phone: 562-981-1202
Toll free: 888-722-2952

Coalition to End Domestic and Sexual Violence
Ventura, CA, Phone: 805-654-8141
Hot line: 805-656-1111
(Spanish) 800-300-2181

CONNECTICUT

Connecticut Coalition Against Domestic Violence
Hartford, CT, Phone: 860-524-5890

Connecticut Sexual Assault Crisis Services
East Hartford, CT, Phone: 860-282-9881

COLORADO

Colorado Coalition Against Sexual Assault
Denver, CO, Phone: 303-861-7033

Colorado Domestic Violence Coalition
Denver, CO, Phone: 303-831-9632
Toll free: 888-778-7091

Colorado Organizations for Victim Assistance
Phone: 303-861-1160

DELAWARE

Rape Crisis
Milford, DE
Phone: 302-422-2078
Wilmington, DE
Phone: 302-761-9100

Delaware Coalition Against Domestic Violence
Wilmington, DE
Phone: 302-658-2958
Bilingual Hot line: 888-522-2571

CONTACT Delaware, Inc.
Wilmington, DE, Phone: 302-761-9800

DISTRICT OF COLUMBIA

D.C. Coalition Against Domestic Violence
Washington, DC, Phone: 202-783-5332

My Sister's Place
Washington, DC, Hot line: 202-529-5991

Rape Crisis Center
Washington, DC, Phone: 202-232-0202 and 202-232-0789

FLORIDA

Florida Coalition Against Domestic Violence
Tallahassee, FL, Phone: 850-425-2749
Toll free: 800-500-1119

Florida Council Against Sexual Violence
Tallahassee, FL, Phone: 850-297-2000

GEORGIA

Georgia Advocates for Battered Women and Children
Atlanta, GA, Phone: 404-524-3847
Toll free: 800-334-2836

Georgia Network to End Sexual Abuse
Atlanta, GA, Phone: 404-659-6482

HAWAII

Hawaii Sex Abuse Treatment Center
Honolulu, HI, Phone: 1-808-535-7600

Hawaii State Coalition Against Domestic Violence
Aiea, HI, Phone: 1-808-486-5072

Sex Abuse Centers Hot Line Numbers
Oahu: 808-524-7273
Maui: 800-890-4318
Kauai:808-245-4144
Big Island, Molokai/Lanai: 808-935-0677

Survivors of Homicide Victims/Drunk Drivers,
Phone: 808-532-623

IDAHO

Idaho Coalition Against Sexual and Domestic Violence
Boise, ID, Phone: 208-384-0419
Toll free: 888-293-6188
Hot line: 800-669-3176

ILLINOIS

Friends of Battered Women and Children
Evanston, IL, Phone: 773-274-5232
Hot line: 800-603-4357

Illinois Coalition Against Domestic Violence
Springfield, IL, Phone: 217-789-2830

Illinois Coalition Against Sexual Assault
Springfield, IL, Phone: 217-753-4117

Life Span
Des Plaines, IL, Phone: 847-824-0382
Hot line: 847-824-4454

INDIANA

Indiana Coalition Against Domestic Violence
Indianapolis, IN, Phone: 317-543-3908
Toll free: 800-332-7385

Indiana Coalition Against Sexual Assault
Indianapolis, IN, Phone: 317-568-4001
Indiana Hot line: 800-334-7233

IOWA

Iowa Coalition Against Domestic Violence
Des Moines, IA, Phone: 515-244-8028
Toll free: 800-942-0333

Iowa Coalition Against Sexual Assault
Des Moines, IA, Phone: 515-244-7424

KANSAS

Kansas Coalition Against Sexual and Domestic Violence
Topeka, KS, Phone: 785-232-9784
Toll free: 888-363-2283

KENTUCKY

Kentucky Domestic Violence Association
Frankfort, KY, Phone: 502-875-4132

Kentucky Association of Sexual Assault Programs
Frankfort, KY, Phone: 502-226-2704

LOUISIANA

Louisiana Coalition Against Domestic Violence
Baton Rouge, LA, Phone: 225-752-1296

Louisiana Foundation Against Sexual Assault
Independence, LA, Phone: 504-747-8815

MAINE

Maine Coalition to End Domestic Violence
Bangor, ME, Phone: 207-941-1194

Maine Coalition Against Sexual Assault
Augusta, ME, Phone: 207-626-0034

MARYLAND

Maryland Coalition Against Sexual Assault
Arnold, MD, Phone: 410-974-4507

Maryland Network Against Domestic Violence
Bowie, MD, Phone: 301-352-4572
Toll Free: 800-634-3577

MASSACHUSETTS

Massachusetts Coalition Against Sexual Assault
and Domestic Violence

Jane Doe Inc., Boston, MA, Phone: 617-248-0902

Massachusetts Coalition of Battered Women
Phone: 617-248-0922

Massachusetts Coalition of Rape Crisis Services
Auburn, MA, Phone: 508-721-9711

Massachusetts Office for Victim Assistance
Phone: 781-727-5200

MICHIGAN

Michigan Coalition Against Domestic and Sexual Violence
Okemos, MI, Phone: 517-347-7000

Bay County Women's Center
Bay City, MI, Phone: 517-686-4551
Toll free: 800-834-2098

Michigan Hot line: 517-265-6776

MINNESOTA

Minnesota Coalition Against Sexual Assault
Minneapolis, MN, Phone: 612-872-7734

Minnesota Coalition for Battered Women
St. Paul, MN, Phone: 651-646-6177
Hot line: 800-646-0994

MISSISSIPPI

Mississippi State Coalition Against Domestic Violence
Jackson, MS, Phone: 601-981-9196
Toll free: 800-898-3234

Mississippi Coalition Against Sexual Assault
Jackson, MS, Phone: 601-987-9011

MISSOURI

Missouri Coalition Against Domestic Violence
Jefferson City, MO, Phone: 314-634-4161

Missouri Coalition Against Sexual Assault
Jefferson City, MO, Phone: 573-636-8776

Missouri Victim Assistance Network
Phone: 800-698-9199

Women's Support and Community Services
St. Louis, MO, Hot line: 314-531-2003

MONTANA

Montana Coalition Against Domestic and Sexual Violence
Helena, MT
Phone: 406-443-7794, Toll free: 1-888-404-7794

Montana Hot line for Domestic and Sexual Violence
Bozeman, MT, Phone: 800-655-7867

Montana State University V.O.I.C.E. Center
Phone: 406-994-7142

University of Montana (S.A.R.S.)
Missoula, MT, Phone: 406-243-4711

NEBRASKA

Nebraska Domestic Violence and Sexual Assault Coalition
Lincoln, NE, Phone: 402-476-6806
Hot line: 800-876-6238

NEVADA

Nevada Network Against Domestic Violence
Reno, NV, Phone: 775-828-1115
Toll free: 800-500-1556

Nevada Coalition Against Sexual Violence
Henderson, NV, Phone: 702-914-6878

SAFE House
Henderson, NV, Phone: 702-451-4203

NEW HAMPSHIRE

New Hampshire Coalition Against Domestic and Sexual Violence
Concord, NH, Phone: 603-224-8893
Toll free: 800-852-3388

NEW JERSEY

New Jersey Coalition Against Sexual Assault
Trenton, NJ, Phone: 609-631-4450

New Jersey Coalition for Battered Women
Trenton, NJ, Phone: 609-584-8107

Strengthen Our Sisters
Hewitt, NJ, Hot line: 973-728-0007

NEW MEXICO

New Mexico State Coalition Against Domestic Violence
Albuquerque, NM, Phone: 505-246-9240
Toll free: 800-773-3645

New Mexico Coalition of Sexual Assault Program
Albuquerque, NM, Phone: 505-883-8020

NEW YORK

New York State Coalition Against Domestic Violence
Albany, NY, Phone: 518-432-4864
Toll free: 800-942-6906

New York State Coalition Against Sexual Assault
Albany, NY, Phone: 518-482-4222

NORTH CAROLINA

North Carolina Coalition Against Domestic Violence
Durham, NC, Phone: 919-956-9124

North Carolina Coalition Against Sexual Assault
Raleigh, NC, Phone: 919-676-7611

NORTH DAKOTA

North Dakota Council on Abused Women's Services
Bismarck, ND, Phone: 701-255-6240
Toll free: 800-472-2911

Rape and Abuse Crisis Center
Fargo, ND, Phone: 701-293-7273

Victim Assistance Program
Grafton, ND, Phone: 701-775-9623

OHIO

Ohio Domestic Violence Network
Columbus, OH, Phone: 614-784-0023
Toll free: 800-934-9840

Ohio Coalition Against Sexual Assault
Columbus, OH, Phone: 614-268-3322

Ohio Victims Services
Columbus, OH, Phone: 614-466-5610

OKLAHOMA

Oklahoma Coalition Against Domestic Violence and Sexual Assault
Phone: 405-848-1815
Toll free: 800-522-9054

OREGON

Oregon Coalition Against Domestic and Sexual Violence
Portland, OR, Phone: 503-223-7411
Toll free: 800-622-3782

Oregon Coalition Against Domestic and Sexual Violence
Salem, OR, Phone: 503-365-9644

PENNSYLVANIA

Laurel House
Norriston, PA
Toll free: 800-642-3150

Pennsylvania Coalition Against Domestic Violence
Phone: 717-545-6400
Toll free: 800-932-4632

Pennsylvania Coalition Against Rape
Enola, PA, Phone: 717-728-9740
Hot line: 800-692-7445

RHODE ISLAND

Rhode Island Coalition Against Domestic and Sexual Violence
Warwick, RI, Phone: 401-467-9943
Toll free: 800-494-8100

SOUTH CAROLINA

South Carolina Coalition Against Domestic Violence and Sexual
Assault
Columbia, SC, Phone: 803-256-2900
Toll free: 800-260-9293

SOUTH DAKOTA

South Dakota Coalition Against Domestic Violence and Sexual
Assault
Pierre, SD, Phone: 605-945-0869
Toll free: 800-572-9196

TENNESSEE

Tennessee Task Force Against Domestic Violence
Nashville, TN, Phone: 615-386-9406
Toll free: 800-356-6767

Tennessee Coalition Against Sexual Assault
Nashville, TN, Phone: 615-259-9055

TEXAS

Texas Association Against Sexual Assault
Austin, TX, Phone: 512-445-1049

Texas Council on Family Violence
Austin, TX, Phone: 512-794-1133
Toll free: 800-525-1978

UTAH

Domestic Violence Advisory Council
Salt Lake City, UT, Phone: 801-538-4100
Toll free: 800-897-5465

Utah Coalition Against Sexual Assault
Salt Lake City, UT, Phone: 801-322-1500

Women Helping Battered Women
Phone: 802-658-1996
Toll free: 800-228-7395

Women's Rape Crisis Center
Toll free: 800-489-7273

VERMONT

Vermont Network Against Domestic Violence and Sexual Assault
Montpelier, VT, Phone: 802-223-6943

VIRGINIA

Virginians Aligned Against Sexual Assault
Charlottesville, VA, Phone: 804-979-9002

Virginians Family Violence and Sexual Assault Hot line
Williamsburg, VA, Phone: 757-221-0990
Toll free: 800-838-8238

WASHINGTON

Washington State Coalition Against Domestic Violence
Lacey, WA
Phone: 360-407-0761

Washington State Domestic Violence Hot line
Toll free: 800-562-6025

Washington Coalition of Sexual Assault Programs
Olympia, WA, Phone: 360-754-7583

WEST VIRGINIA

West Virginia Foundation for Rape Information and Services
Fairmont, WV, Phone: 304-366-9500

West Virginia Coalition Against Domestic Violence
Charleston, WV, Phone: 304-965-3552

WISCONSIN

Manitowoc Domestic Violence Center
Manitowoc, WI, Phone: 920-684-5770

Wisconsin Coalition Against Domestic Violence
Madison, WI, Phone: 608-255-0539

Wisconsin Coalition Against Sexual Assault
Madison, WI, Phone: 608-257-1516

WYOMING

Wyoming Coalition Against Domestic Violence and Sexual Assault
Laramie, WY, Phone: 307-755-5481
Toll free: 800-990-3877

NATIONAL CONTACTS

National Center for Victims of Crime (NCVC)
Phone: 800-394-2255
(Referrals to victim services in local areas)

National Clearinghouse for Alcohol and Drug Information
Toll free number: 800-729-6686

National Coalition Against Domestic Violence
Washington, DC
Phone: 703-765-0339

National Coalition Against Sexual Assault
Harrisburg, PA
Phone: 717-232-7460
(Promotes victim services and referrals to local support services.)

National Criminal Justice Reference Service (NCJRS)
General Information
Toll free number: 800-851-3420

Office for Victims of Crime
Toll free number: 800-627-6872

Office of National Drug Control Policy
Toll free number: 800-666-3332

National Domestic Violence Hot line
Toll free number: 800-799-7233
TDD: 800-787-3224

National Network to End Domestic Violence
Washington, DC
Phone: 202-543-5566

National Organization for Victim Assistance (NOVA)
Washington, DC
Phone: 800-879-6682
(Offers information pertaining to rape and domestic violence support groups)

National Resource Center on Domestic Violence
Phone: 800-537-2238
(Coordinates domestic violence information, resource development and technical help.)

National Sexual Violence Resource Center (NSVRC)
Enola, PA
Phone: 877-739-3895 and 717-909-0710

National Victim Center
New York, NY
Phone: 212-753-6880

Office for Victims of Crime
Washington, DC
Phone: 202-3-7-5983
Rape Abuse and Incest National Network

RAINN Hot line
Phone: 800-656-4673
(Helps locate local resources such as counseling, shelters)

Security On Campus, Inc.
Web site: http://www.campussafety.org/resources/victimassistance□

CONTACTS FOR FRAUD

(To include resource information for Internet fraud and Identity Theft)

Consumer Protection Agency
Web site: www.consumer.gov/idtheft/

Credit Report Centers

Equifax Credit Report Center
To report fraud: 800-525-6285
Request credit report: 800-685-1111
Web site: www.equifax.com

Experian Credit Report Center
Phone: 800-397-3742
Web site: http://www.experian.com

Trans Union Credit Report Center
To report fraud: 800-680-7289
Request credit report: 800-916-8800
Web site: http://www.tuc.com

DMA Mail Preference Service
P.O. Box 9014
Farmingdale, NY 11735-9008
(Contact address to remove your name from direct mail lists)

DMA Telephone Preference Service
P.O. Box 9014
Farmingdale, NY 11735-9014
(Contact address to remove your name from direct phone lists)

Direct email web site: http://www.e-mps.org
(Email address to have your name removed from direct email lists)

Department of Justice
Web site: http://www.usdoj.gov

Federal Bureau of Investigations
Web site: http://www.fbi.gov
(Local phone books list regional offices in the blue section)

Internal Revenue Service
Tax fraud: 800-829-0433
Web site: http://www.treas.gov/irs/ci

Federal Trade Commission
Address: 600 Pennsylvania Avenue, NW
Washington, DC 20580
Phone: 877-438-4338
Web site: http://www.consumer.gov
(The Federal Trade Commission works to prevent fraud and unfair business practices. The FTC also provides consumers with crime prevention information. Complaints of fraudulent acts can be reported either by giving the complainant's name or anonymously, if preferred.)

National Fraud Information Center
Toll free number: 800-876-7060
(Telemarketing and Internet fraud)

Social Security Administration
Fraud Hot line: 800-269-0271
Web site: http://www.ssa.gov

United States Postal Inspection Service
Web site: http://www.usps.gov/websites/depart/inspect
(Identify theft involving U.S. mail)

OTHER HELPFUL RESOURCES

Mothers Against Drunk Driving (MADD)
Toll free number: 800-FYI-CALL

Men Stopping Rape (Community-based program)
Madison, WI, Phone: 608-257-4444

Parents of Murdered Children (POMC)
Phone: 513-721-5683

North-American Inter-fraternity Conference Web site: http://www. nicindy.org
(Latest Greek issues and links to NIC web sites.)

Safe Campus Now
Athens, GA
Phone: 706-354-1115
(Managed by students and community volunteers for Florida, Georgia, and Tennessee)

State Hazing Laws
Web site: http://www.stophazing.org

OTHER RESOURCE WEB SITES

Alfred University National Hazing Study
Web site: http://www.alfred.edu

AT&T Internet list of personal names, phone numbers and addresses
Web site: http://www.anywho.com

Bureau of Justice Statistics (BJS)
Web site: www.ojp.usdoj.gov

Chronicle of Higher Education (drug and alcohol violations on U. S. college campuses)
http://www.chronicle.com/free/v45/i38/38a00101

Duke University (study on alcohol and drugs)
Web site: http://www.mc.duke.edu/h-devil/drugs/at-duke.htm

Federal Campus Security and Crime Statistics
Web site: http://www.ope.edu.gov/security

Highway Loss Data Institute
Web site: www.insure.com

Harvard School of Public Health
http://www.hsph.harvard.edu

Identity Theft information
Web site: http://www.ftc.gov/bcp/conline/pubs/credit4/idtheft.htm

Safe Dating on the Internet
Web site: http://www.saferdating.com

EPILOGUE:

BRINGING IT ALL TOGETHER IN
SEVENTEEN RULES

Review and practice the safety guides provided for you in this book. To recap some important rules, remember and practice the following seventeen rules:

17 Safety Smart Student Rules

1. Be familiar with who and what is around you. Always be aware.

2. Maintain a healthy lifestyle and be confident.

3. Choose a college that is committed to your safety and security.

4. Become a participant in protecting your personal safety.

5. Assess the safety factors where you live, to include both inside and outside your home.

6. Keep your doors and windows locked.

7. Park and walk in well-lit areas. Walk with a friend whenever possible and avoid being alone in isolated, dark areas.

8. Protect your personal identify and property.

9. When using the Internet, protect your personal information. Be cautious of others and alert about their motives.

10. Report suspicious persons, activities, and crimes to police officials.

11. Protect yourself and your dwelling. Do not allow intruders and strangers to roam around your dorm, apartment or home.

12. Abide to traffic laws and travel in a courteous and safe manner.

13. Never get into a vehicle with an unfamiliar acquaintance or stranger.

14. Never allow anyone to abuse you, and do not allow anyone to have power and control over you.

15. Do not use illegal drugs and abuse alcohol.

16. Women, learn to clearly say "no" to a man if you do not want to have sex; and men, honor and abide to her "no." Communicate with each other.

17. Get professional help when you are a victim of rape, stalking, domestic violence, or any other personally violent victimization. Do not handle it alone. Familiarize yourself with helpful resources provided in this book and in your community.

If you follow these seventeen rules while attending college and throughout your life, you will reduce your chances of becoming a victim of crime. Learn these safety rules and when particular situations or problems arise, consult the safety guidelines, information and helpful resources given in this book.

You are at the center of your life's journey. How well you manage your mental, physical and personal safety fitness will determine the quality of your life. No one should ever gain power and control over you. **Be strong, be aware, be confident and be safety smart.**

REFERENCES

Brewer, James D. The Danger From Strangers. New York: Plenum Press, 1994.

Ferguson, Robert and Jeanine. A Guide to Rape Awareness and Prevention. Wethersfield, CT: Turtle Press, 1994.

Foundation for Crime Prevention Education. Safe, Smart and Self-Reliant. Rockville, Maryland: Safety Press. 1996.

Marrewa, Al. The Feminine Warrior. New York: Kensington Publishing Corp., 1998.

McKay, Davis, and Patrick Fanning. How To Communicate. New York: MJF Books, 1983.

Meloy, J. Reid. The Psychology of Stalking. San Diego, California: Academic Press, 1998.

Michaud, Stephen G. and Hugh Aynesworth. Ted Bundy, Conversations with a Killer. New York: NAL Books, 1989.

Motley, James B. Protect Yourself, Your Family, Your Home. New York: Brassey's, 1994.

NiCarthy, Ginny and Sue Davidson. You Can Be Free. Seattle, Washington:
The Seal Press, 1989.

Philpin, John and John Donnelly. Beyond Murder. New York: Penguin Books, 1994.

Shuker-Haines, Frances. Everything You Need to Know About Date Rape.
New York: The Rosen Publishing Group, 1990.

Snow, Robert L. Stopping a Stalker. New York: Plenum Press, 1998.

Sommer, Barone, and Anna Harabin Marltz. Psycho-Cybernetics 2000.
New Jersey: Prentice Hall, 1993.

Spence-Diehl, Emily. Stalking, A Handbook for Victims. Holmes Beach, Florida: Learning Publications, Inc. 1999.

The National Insurance Crime Bureau. Florida Auto Theft Intelligence Unit, Auto Theft Journal, Volume 18, January - March 2001.

Wechsler, Nelson, and Elissa Weitzman. "From Knowledge to Action". How Harvard's College Alcohol Study Can Help Your Campus Design a Campaign Against Student Alcohol Abuse. January/February 2000.

Government Agency Web Sites

Federal Bureau of Investigations Uniform Crime Reporting/National Incident-Based Reporting System Crime Definitions, Excerpted from the Implementing Regulations of the Campus Security Act Federal Register, April 29, 1994, Vol. 59, No. 82. Web site http://nces.ed.gov/pbus/97402-a.html

Federal Office of the Status of Women (OSW), "Against the Odds: How Women Survive Domestic Violence." Executive Summary by Keys Young, August 1998, Web site: http://www.osw.dpmc.gov.au/content/publications/keysum.html

The Ninth Special Report to the U. S. Congress on Alcohol and Health. "Charting Recent Progress, Advances in Alcohol Research". Lori A. Wolfgang. Vol. 21, No. 4, 1997.
United States. Bureau of Justice Statistics (BJS). Web site, http://www.ojp.usdoj.gov

United States. Executive Office of the President. Office of National Drug Control

Policy, Drug Policy Information Clearinghouse Fact Sheet. "Gamma Hydroxybutyrate (GHB) November 1999. Web site: http://www.whitehousedrugpolicy.gov

United States. Executive Office of the President. Office of National Drug Control Policy. Drug Policy Information Clearinghouse Fact Sheet.
"MDMA". July 2000.
Web site: http://www.whitehousedrugpolicy.gov

United States. Executive Office of the President. Office of National Drug Control Policy. Drug Policy Information Clearinghouse Fact Sheet.
"Rohypnol". June 1998.

United States. U. S. Department of Justice, Office of Justice Programs, Bureau of Statistics.
"Intimate Partner Violence." 2000. Web site, http://www.ojp.usdoj.gov/bjs/pub/ascii/ipv.txt

United States. U. S. Department of Justice, Office of Justice Programs, Bureau of Statistics.
Age Patterns of Victims of Serious Violent Crime. September 1997, NCJ-162031. Web site, http://www.ojp.usdoj.gov/bjs/pub/ascii/apvsvc.txt

United States. U. S. Department of Justice, Office of Justice Programs, Bureau of Statistics.
The 1995 Survey of Campus Law Enforcement Agencies.
Web site, http://www.ojp.usdoj.gov/bjs/pub/ascii/clea95.txt

United States. U. S. Department of Justice, Office of Justice Programs, Bureau of Justice Statistics. Drugs & Crime Data. "Fact Sheet: Drug-Related Crime". September 1994: NCJ-149286.

United States. U. S. Department of Justice, National Institute of Justice. Web site, http://www.ojp.usdoj.gov/nij

United States. U.S. Department of Justice, Drug Enforcement Administration,
"Cocaine". Web site, http://www.usdoj.gov/dea/concern/cocaine.htm

United States. U.S. Department of Justice, Drug Enforcement Administration
"Drug Use in the United States." Web site, http://www.usdoj.gov/dea/concern/use.htm

United States. U. S. Department of Justice, Drug Enforcement Administration. Mathias, Robert.
"Ecstasy" "Damages the Brian and Impairs Memory in Humans". Web site, http://www.usdoj.gov/dea/concern/mdma/ecstasy02077.htm

United States. U. S. Department of Justice, Drug Enforcement Administration.
"Gamma Hydroxybutyrate" (GHB). Web site, http://www.usdoj.gov/dea/concern/ghb.htm

United States. U. S. Department of Justice, Drug Enforcement Administration.
"Heroin". Web site, http://www.usdoj.gov/dea/concern/heroin.htm

United States. U. S. Department of Justice, Drug Enforcement Administration.
"Ketamine". Web site, http://www.usdoj.gov/dea/concern/ketamine.htm

United States. U. S. Department of Justice, Drug Enforcement Administration.
"Lysergic Acid Diethylamide (LSD). Web site, http://www.usdoj.gov/dea/concern/lsd.htm

United States. U.S. Department of Justice, Drug Enforcement Administration,
"Marijuana". Web site,
http://www.usdoj.gov/dea/concern/marijuana.htm

United States. U.S. Department of Justice, Drug Enforcement Administration,
"Methamphetamine (Meth)". Web site,
http://www.usdoj.gov/dea/concern/meth.htm

United States. U.S. Department of Justice, Drug Enforcement Administration,
"Phencyclidine" (PCP). Web site,
http://www.usdoj.gov/dea/concern/pcp.htm

United States. U.S. Department of Justice, Drug Enforcement Administration,
"Rohypnol". Web site,
http://www.usdoj.gov/dea/concern/rohypnol.htm

United States. U.S. Department of Justice, Drug Enforcement Administration
"Methylphenidate" (Ritalin). Web site,
http://www.usdoj.gov/dea/concern/ritalin.htm

United States. U.S. Department of Justice, Violence Against Women Office. "Rural Domestic Violence and Child Victimization Enforcement Grants".
Web site, http://www.ojp.usdoj.gov/vawo/grants/rural/descrip.htm

United States. U.S. Department of Justice, Violence Against Women Office. "Subtitle B— Safe Homes for Women". Web site,
http://www.ojp.usdoj.gov/vawo/laws/vawa/stitle_b.htm

United States. U.S. Department of Justice, Violence Against Women Office. "The Violence Against Women Act: Breaking the Cycle of Violence".
Web site http://www.ojp.usdoj.gov/vawo/laws/cycle.htm

Organization and University Web Sites

APB Safety Center, Web site,
http://www.apbnews.com/safetycenter/family/campus

AT&T Internet Resource, Web site, http://www.anywho.com

Federal Campus Security and Crime Statistics, Web site,
http://www.ope.edu.gov/security

Fox News. Web site,
http://www.foxnews.com/national/082400/campuscrime_mand.sml

Highway Loss Data Institute Study. Web site,
http://www.insure.com

Indiana Daily Student. Web site,
http://www.idsnews.com/news/2000.02.25/campus/2000.02.25.clery.html

Nation & World. Web site,
http://seattletimes.nwsource.com/news/nation-world/htm198/booz04_20000604.html

Rape Abuse and Incest National Network (Rainn). Web site,
http://www.rainn.org

Security On Campus, Inc. Web site, http://www.campussafety.org

The Anti-stalking Web Site, http://www.antistalking.com

The Chronicle of Higher Education, "Drug and Alcohol Violations on U. S. College Campuses. Web site, http://www.chronicle.com/free/v45/i38/38a00101

The Chronicle of Higher Education. "Shift in Crime-Reporting Law Fails to End Debate Over Accuracy of Statistics" by Julie L. Nicklin. June 9, 2000. Web site http://chronicle.com/free/v46/i40/40a05001.htm

The Stalking Assistance Site. Web site, http://www.stalkingassistance.com

Alfred University's National Study on Hazing. Web site, http://www.alfred.edu

Duke University, "Drugs and Alcohol, Alcohol at Duke". Web site, http://h-devil-www.mc.duke.edu/h-devil/drugs/at-duke.htm

Harvard School of Public Health 1999, College Alcohol Study Web site, http://www.hsph.harvard.edu/Organizations/cas/test/rpt2000/CAS2000rpt.shtml

University of Illinois at Urbana-Champaign, McKinley Health Center, Alcohol Study. Web site, http://www.mckinley.uiuc.edu/health-info/drug-alc/alc-effe.html

INDEX

T

U

V

W

About the Author:

Colleen Kenniston, writer, educator, and police investigator is engaged in personal safety education for high school and college students. She is a Florida certified police investigator. For 12 years, Kenniston has helped hundreds of college students who are victims or witnesses of non-violent and violent crimes. She has specialized training in national safe schools issues, residential security, domestic violence and sexual assault. Her executive management articles have been featured in the *Florida Police Chief Magazine*. Kenniston has a Bachelor's Degree in Sociology and a Master's Degree in Organizational Management. She is also a professor of business for Columbia Southern University. She lives in Gainesville, Florida and secondary residence in Murphy, North Carolina. She has one son, Jason Kendall. To inquire more about college student safety issues, readers can email her at ckenniston3@cs.com.

www.ingramcontent.com/pod-product-compliance
Lightning Source LLC
Chambersburg PA
CBHW030307290526
45785CB00001B/242